Johanna Jones has lived in the Isle ̣ince the 1950s and in that time has continuousı̣ ̣een engaged in the educational and cultural life of the Island. Her work as a lecturer for the Adult Education Department of Southampton University and the Workers' Educational Association led to studies in Island social history especially in the lives of rural workers over the past two hundred years. The history of farmhouses and cottages became a major study and she has recently completed a description of all the farmhouses, farm buildings and farm lands on the Swainston estate in 1630. A council member of the Isle of Wight Natural History and Archaeological Society, a committee member of the Isle of Wight Buildings Preservation Trust and a Trustee of Carisbrooke Castle Museum she continues her active interest in Island life.

ISLE OF WIGHT BEDSIDE BOOK

A Collection of Prose and Poetry

SELECTED AND INTRODUCED BY
JOHANNA JONES

THE DOVECOTE PRESS

First published in 2004 by
The Dovecote Press Ltd
Stanbridge, Wimborne, Dorset BH21 4JD

ISBN 1 904349 36 6

Introduction © Johanna Jones 2004

Typeset in Monotype Sabon
Printed and bound by The Baskerville Press Ltd
Salisbury, Wiltshire

All papers used by The Dovecote Press are natural,
recyclable products made from wood grown in sustainable,
well-managed forests.

A CIP catalogue record for this book is available
from the British Library

1 3 5 7 9 8 6 4 2

CONTENTS

INTRODUCTION

When I began work on this collection of prose and poetry a friend asked me if it would have illustrations and I replied, 'No'. But immediately, and more so as I worked on it, that answer was shown to be completely wrong. The book is full of pictures of the best kind; descriptions and experiences brought to life by the people who were there, telling us what they saw and felt.

Landscape and seascape must claim a large part of the whole as these are so special to the Island, combining romantic and dramatic scenery in so small a space, a duality that determined the Island's future as a holiday resort. Agriculture was the mainstay of the local economy for the greater part of our local history and there is plentiful evidence to show how changes in farming methods brought change to the landscape.

People make a community and many of them speak here. The visitors who left enthusiastic comments, those who had dire experiences in trying to get across to the Island and those who sailed happily into port have their own views, as do the holiday visitors and those who provided for them. The Royal Family, the Tennyson family, a humble pauper, servants in a large country house, the farmer's wife, the farm labourer, all have their personal pictures to give us. Cowes Week fashionables, the Excise officer and the smuggler, all have their say.

I thank my longstanding friends for their help and suggestions in preparing this book; Roy Brinton, Bob West, Charles Taylor, Diana Harding, and my husband Jack. The use of the library in Carisbrooke Castle Museum was much appreciated as was the assistance from the County Record Office. The ever-helpful staff in the reference library of the Lord Louis Library, Newport, have my grateful thanks for their friendly response to my many visits. Finally, many thanks to Elizabeth and David for converting my manuscript into a readable form and bringing the whole thing to fruition.

A bedside book should send you happily to sleep or comfort you if awake in the early morning hours and I hope this pot-pourri of Island life and times will have that effect - and that it will send you to read the sources from which they are taken.

JOHANNA JONES *October 2004*

I · PRELUDE

An Invitation to the Isle of Wight

(To the Rev. D. Maurice)

Come, when no graver cares employ
Godfather, come and see your boy:
      Your presence will be sun in winter,
Making the little one leap for joy.

For, being of that honest few,
Who give the Fiend himself his due,
      Should eighty-thousand college-councils
Thunder 'Anathema' at you;

Should all our churchmen foam in spite
At you, so careful of the right,
      Yet one lay-hearth would give you welcome
(Take it and come to the Isle of Wight);

Where, far from noise and smoke of town,
I watch the twilight falling brown
      All round a careless-ordered garden
Close to the ridge of a noble down.

You'll have no scandal while you dine,
But honest talk and wholesome wine,
    And only hear the magpie gossip
Garrulous under a roof of pine:

For groves of pine on either hand,
To break the blast of winter, stand;
    And further on, the hoary Channel
Tumbles a billow on chalk and sand;

Where, if below the milky steep
Some ship of battle slowly creep
    And on thro' zones of light and shadow
Glimmer away to the lonely deep,

We might discuss the Northern sin
Which made a selfish war begin;
    Dispute the claims, arrange the chances;
Emperor, Ottoman, which shall win:

Or whether war's avenging rod
Shall lash all Europe into blood;
    Till you shall turn to dearer matters,
Dear to the man who is dear to God;

How best to help the slender store,
How mend the dwellings of the poor;
    How gain in life, as life advances,
Valour and charity more and more.

Come, Maurice, come: the lawn as yet
Is hoar with rime, or spongy wet;
    But when the wreath of March has
blossom'd
Crocus, anemone, violet,

Or later, pay one visit here,
For those are few we hold as dear;
    Nor pay but one, but come for many
Many and many a happy year.
Alfred Lord Tennyson, January (1854)

2 · THE ISLAND LANDSCAPE

An Island is Born

Wight was not always an Island. Until well after the last Ice Age it was physically joined to what is now the Hampshire coast, and its separation was the result of post-glacial changes in sea levels and the consequent marine breaching of a continuous chalk barrier of which the Purbeck downs and the Island's central spine ridge are surviving sections. These are now separated by a sea gap of nearly twenty miles with the Old Harry Rocks and the Needles as their respective outlying fragments. This chalk barrier completed the south side of the Hampshire syncline and protected an area of low-lying Tertiary deposits, now submerged as Bournemouth Bay, against wave attack and other forms of erosion.

The basin was drained eastwards by the so-called 'Solent River' which may be regarded as a southern counterpart of the Thames. It was fed by many sizeable tributaries, the most distant now lying within the borders of modern Somerset. From the north the 'Solent' received the ancestors of rivers such as the Test, Stour, Avon and Itchen, whilst its tributaries from the south were the now diminutive Isle of Wight rivers whose courses, on account of the land lying south of its present shores, were then more extensive. Today the old course of the 'Solent River' is represented by the Dorset Frome and by the Solent and Spithead straits.

The chronology of the final breakthrough of the chalk ridge is still a matter of controversy. Britain became physically detached from the

European continent somewhere around 6000-7000 BC and though some authorities place the event much later, it is highly probable that the Isle of Wight received its own insularity about the same time. The date is of geological significance only, for the outcome was the same – the creation of what came to be a diamond-shaped island of some 155 square miles (397 sq km) with a maximum length of 23 miles (35km) from the Needles in the west to Bembridge Foreland in the east, and a maximum width of 13 miles (21km) from Egypt Point at Cowes to St Catherine's Point in the south.

The Solent and Spithead which separate it from the Hampshire coast, meet at Cowes Road to form the deep inlet leading to Southampton Water up which the world's largest ships can easily proceed. The shelter afforded by the Isle of Wight played an important part in the development of this historic waterway but contrary to popular belief it is not responsible for the freak bonus of double tides which have made Southampton and Portsmouth the maritime centres they are. The tides, which also affect the Island ports of Yarmouth, Cowes and, to a lesser extent, Newport, are the result of up-channel tidal surges meeting those coming down-channel from the North Sea. The Venerable Bede almost had it right. 'In this sea', he states, 'comes a double tide out of the seas which spring from the infinite ocean of the Arctic which surrounds all Britain'.

Brian Dicks, The Isle of Wight, (1979)

A Land of Varied Soils

Even to a casual observer, the landscape of the Isle of Wight is made up of contrasting areas. The first recorded observation was made by John Camden in the later sixteenth century:

> Through the midst thereof runs a long tract or
> chaine of hills, yeilding plentie of pasture, and
> forrage for sheepe. The wool of which, next unto
> that of Lemster and Coteswold is esteemed best,
> and in speciall request with clothiers, whereby
> there groweth to the inhabitants much gaine and
> profit: the North part is all over greene with
> meddows, pastures and woods: the South side

lieth wholly in manner, bedecked with cornefields
enclosed, where at each end the sea on the North–
side doth emboseme, encroach within it selfe, that
it makes the almost two Islands *(Camden 1637)*

*Over two centuries later, the view from Ashey Down on the lateral
'chaine of hills' was described by John Albin* [author of the *History of
the Isle of Wight*, 1799], *who also mentioned the chalk downland in the
south of the island :*

On this elevated spot are the most extensive views of Portsmouth,
Gosport, Southampton Water, Spithead, St Helens and the harbour
of Brading; the rich woods around Nunwell and to Wootton Bridge,
on the east and north side, and on the south, the fertile vale of
Newchurch and Arreton, extending to the hills of Shanklin, Wroxall,
Week, and St Catherines *(Albin 1799)*

*A visitor to the island a few years before Albin also commented on the
great variety of soil types to be found:*

The variation of the soil of this island is beyond description. They
must be truly termed the vagaries of nature . . . *(Hassell 1790)*
John Margham, Charters, landscapes and hides on the Isle of Wight, (2003)

Ancient Woodland

The northern half of the Island is studded with ancient woodlands . . .
Some fine old woods extend down to a natural shoreline adjoining tidal
marshes, as they must have done for hundreds of years. This is well seen
around sheltered inlets at Newtown and Wootton Creek. Remains of
oak trunks and roots embedded in the intertidal muds between Ryde and
Wootton have been radiocarbon dated back to 3000-4000 BC, providing
evidence that at one time these woodlands extended much further out
from the current coastline, and marine erosion continues to erode the
wooded cliffs . . .

Parkhurst is a fascinating woodland complex with affinities to the
New Forest, and it is the largest forest on an ancient site on the Island.
Even so, it represents only a fragment of the extent of the former Royal

hunting forest, which in medieval times seems to have extended westward towards Swainston. The area was gradually reduced by enclosures and in its present extent dates principally from the 1812 Enclosure Act . . . In the early decades of the nineteenth century, much of Parkhurst Forest was replanted with oak, including Sessile Oak. In the twentieth century, plantations of conifers have heavily modified the landscape, Nevertheless, a great deal of interest survives. Around Mark's Corner, at the north end of the forest, ancient pasture woodland dominated by Sessile Oak, Beech and Holly can be seen.

Wood pasture was managed woodland in which farm animals or deer were allowed to graze. Although historic documents suggest that livestock were often not effectively excluded from recently cut coppice, proper working wood pasture appears to have been scarce on the Island, and none survives today.

Colin Pope, The Isle of Wight Flora, (2003)

The Chalk Downs

The chalk downs running from west to east, from the Needles to Whitecliff Bay are the backbone of the Island, their whiteness concealed by green turf which man, not nature, has contrived.

In recent, Stone Age times, after the Ice Ages and the Woolly Mammoths had retreated, the then islanders slowly felled the forest that clothed the downs and began to graze beasts along their length. Generation upon generation of cropping teeth suppressed the climax vegetation and nurtured a priceless turf of grasses, milkwort, restharrow, dwarf thistle, thyme, red valerian, horseshoe and kidney vetch, quinancywort, fairy flax, centaury, eyebright, lesser quaking grass, and many more, including among a rich repertoire of orchids, lady's tresses. The spine became a sheep-walk patrolled by shepherds and their flocks of Dorset sheep. Mainland ewes were shipped across to lamb early in mild Island pastures. Sheep, by consuming a rich resource, preserve it: they shear the monuments left by our ancestors and present them clean against the sky; their exploitation is conservation.

Where the turf is founded upon angular flint, capping the chalk, it puts up clumps of furze and bramble, and gnarled hawthorn trees that seem petrified in a perpetual gale. A gravelly track runs before

Brighstone Forest; below, marl pits, like those that pock the downs from east to west and limed the land from north to south, display old wounds; and, like all the springs that tap the spine's reservoir, Buddlebrook runs out at Buddle Hole and skirts the site of Rock Roman Villa and the quarry at Coombe . . .

The broad crown of Bowcombe Down ripples with furrows. From here you see across the *beau combe* to the rumpled patchwork cushion of Garston Down; and beyond, across the Wilderness and the Bowl of the Island to the answering chalk bulwark of the Southern Downs, poised above the Channel.'

Paul Hyland, Wight: Biography of an Island, (1997)

Maxwell Gray – Mary Gleed Tuttiett – was born in Newport, the daughter of a Newport doctor. Her major work, The Silence of Dean Maitland, *published in 1906, was the novel of the year and made her a world bestseller. The story still reads well today, with a theme of unresolved love between a local girl and the son of the manor, the tragedy this brought about and, unlike Thomas Hardy, a conclusion that was satisfactory to all. Her tale opens in the village of Calbourne, thinly disguised as Chalkburne, and includes a description of the scenery on the road between Carisbrooke and that village. In every respect it would serve as a guide today.*

Here, where the enclosed land ended, was a five-barred gate in the mild hedgerow. The grey fallows and wan stubble-fields sloped swiftly away from the gate to a bottom of verdant pastures dotted with trees and homesteads; beyond them were more dim fields, and then a wide belt of forest, principally firs . . .

To the left of it stretched a wide champaign, rich in woodland, and bounded in the far distance by two chalky summits, at whose steep bases surged the unseen sea. Here and there in the breaks of wood and forest on the horizon, Alma's accustomed eyes saw some grey touches which in bright summer were tiny bays of sapphire sea.

Now they are at the summit of the steep hill. On one side is dense coppice; on the other Swaynstone Park slopes down in woodland, glade and park-like meadow to the sea-bounded horizon.

They have just passed the entrance-gates of Swaynstone – lonely gates, unfurnished with a lodge – and the waggon stops at some smaller gates on the other side of the road, where the upland still rises, not in bare down, but in rich meadow, to a hanging wood, out of which peeps dimly in the dusk a small white structure, built with colonnade supporting architrave, to imitate a Greek temple – Alma's home.

Maxwell Gray, The Silence of Dean Maitland, (*1906*)

Undoubtedly, the most dramatic and wild area in the Island was the Undercliff. More comments were made by visitors and writers on this part of the Island than any other, and yet it was extraordinarily difficult to get there until the railway came to Ventnor. The few roads for coach travel crossed wild upland heath, but when the intrepid traveller arrived the scene he saw was worth the discomfort. Much of this was due to its enclosure between the sea and high cliffs a little way inland. In 1611 John Speed named the area from Bonchurch to Niton 'St. Laurence Park', but with its rough land and tumbled rocks it still looked as it had been in medieval times, not a park but an open chase for hunting.

The Road from St. Laurence to Niton

The scenery along the road is now of the most enchanting description; the undulating character of the ground breaks the sameness of the picture, and calls forth new beauties at every turn. The woody dells by which the road is bounded on the northern side affords a shelter to the numerous nightingales with which this locality abounds. Soon after passing an entrance gate to the left, and which leads to Old Park, we enter a most lovely part of our route.

The broken foreground on our right, covered with its velvet herbage, its bold masses of rock and miniature dells and brakes, backed by the towering cliffs, renders it a scene replete with beauty, whilst, on the left, the bright foliage of its wooded glens, extending to the very strand, with the deep blue sea beyond them, form a prospect of surpassing loveliness.

After reaching the summit of the hill in this broken ground, through which the road winds, 'Puckaster Cove', with its little fishing huts and boats is seen to the left, and on the right is the foot-track leading to 'Cripple Path', a steep ascent, by which the upper part of the cliff is gained, which is here, probably, between one hundred and two hundred feet in height.

George A. Martin, M.D., The Undercliff of the Isle of Wight, (*1849*)

Once into Niton there remained one final dramatic scene to view. A long pull up the lower part of St. Catherine's Down and the approach to Black Gang Chine could be seen. This was already a commercial attraction, if in a rather subtle way, as Dr. Martin discovered. It remains so today, although the sea has now stolen almost all the land the nineteenth century traveller saw.

. . . after passing the [Black Gang Chine Hotel] we arrived at a little cottage, converted into a sort of bazaar, through which lies the path leading down to the Chine. A long building on the right hand, situated on the premises, contains a skeleton of a whale which was cast on shore in a dying state, near the Needles, four or five years since. The proprietor of this little bazaar and exhibition rents the Chine, and, although no charge is made to visitors for the privilege of using the pathway, which is renewed every year at no little cost, owing to the frequent falling of rock in the winter season, yet they are generally expected to make a trifling purchase on their return.

George A. Martin, M.D., The Undercliff of the Isle of Wight, (*1849*)

The local Directory prepared visitors for the scene they might expect.

The traveller is now approaching a most tremendous chasm; a wondrous work of the all-governing hand of divine power. Black Gang Chine here terminates the Undercliffe, and is by some considered the most interesting and attractive feature of the Island. The extreme edge of St. Catherine's Hill overhangs this ponderous and natural excavation, and is from eight to nine hundred feet above the level of the sea; from this immense height, in fine weather the coast of Dorset is plainly visible. Elevated above the waters, and looking down upon the dread abyss below, the spectator views the surrounding wild and terrific masses with awe and admiration. Frowningly the rocks seem to warn the foundering mariner from its gloomy shores, but in vain; the desolating and destroying winds will force upon these frightful rocks, the shattered bark, where destruction but too often waits the hapless crew . . .

Lambert's Directory (*1839*)

3 · SOME VISITORS

Idiosyncratically, I want to begin this section on visitors to the Island with one who didn't come but very much wanted to.

Queen Elizabeth I

Queen Elizabeth travelled widely during the summer months to many parts of her kingdom but she never visited the Isle of Wight. How nearly she came to making a visit is revealed by Sir Robert Cecil, who was travelling with her. At the end of August 1591 she was in Portsmouth where she watched martial sports in which men from the Island took part, and when she moved on to Southampton she determined to visit her cousin Sir George Carey, the governor of the Island, living with his wife at Carisbrooke Castle. However, Carey intervened with a dash across the Solent, clearly alarmed at the prospect of this impromptu royal visit. Cecil's correspondence with the Lord Chancellor tells the tale.

Sir Robert Cecil to Lord Chancellor Hatton 4 Sept. 1591
'now her Majestie is determined, without possibility of change, to goe to the isle of Weight to bedd on Munday night with very few in a pynnace of her owne to dyne att Cawshott which is X miles by sea and from thence after dynner to the landing place called Cowes and so to bedd at the castle and to tarry there but a night . . .'

6 Sept. 1591

' . . . This was the day appointed and sette downe for the queen to goe to the Ilande, and so continewed firmly till yestreday night att 6 of the clock, that Sir George Carye came thither, who expressed the length of the journey and the uncertainy of the winde, which must for her Majestie's purpose bee one way going and another comeinge, for else might shee have stayed longer than shee would. By this and other circumstances her Majestie's purpose is altered and homeward. According to my last jestes[plans for the queen's future lodgings], she doth tomorrow take her journey, not finding herselfe very well disposed and troubled with a cold.'

ed. Ian W. Archer, Religion, Politics, and Society in Sixteenth Century England, (2003)

William Schellinks visits Newport 1662

Schellinks, a Dutch visitor, crossed to the Island from Southampton on 12 September. The following day the Bishop of Winchester arrived at Cowes and was escorted to Newport where he was to hold a confirmation service. These were rare occasions and many people attended the service. Schellinks determined to be there, but, compared to the serious and sober Lutheran confirmations, he was astonished at what he saw.

On the 14th September in the morning we were ferried over by Benjamin Newland's boat to East Cowes, where all the dwellings and warehouses were built by him. This Mr. Benjamin Newland has a very fine house there, and warehouses and wharves for building and repairing ships etc.

We were entertained with an excellent breakfast at his house, and after that we crossed over and rode again to Newport. When we got there we went to the church; the service was over and the Bishop proceeded with the confirmation of the people and blessing by laying on of hands: there was such an immense crowd of people who, without any order, jostled each other as if to get money.

Note When I saw every Tom, Dick, and Harry was confirmed by the Bishop by the hundred without any examination or distinction, I joined the end of the crowd and pushed into the choir and received the blessing from Bishop Morley of Winchester.

eds. Maurice Exwood and H.L. Lehman, The Journal of William Schellinks' Travels in England 1661-1663, (1993)

John Wesley visits Shorwell

Wesley made several visits to the Island, chiefly concentrating on Newport as the main town, but in October 1753 he went out to Shorwell and is unusual in actually commenting on the inland scene.

Wed. Oct. 3 1753

A little before noon we set out for Shorwell, a village six miles from Newport. I never saw a more fruitful, or more pleasant country than the inland part of this Island. About one, I preached at Shorwell to, I suppose, all the poor and middling people of the town. I believe some of the rich also designed to come, but something of more importance – a dinner – came between.

John B. Dyson, Methodism in the Isle of Wight, *(1865)*

A Poet comes to Carisbrooke

John Keats was twenty-two years old when he came to the Island in 1817. He had been encouraged by his brothers to improve his health by visiting the country and on 15 April he left Southampton for Cowes. Two days later he was settled in Mrs Cook's house in New Village, a housing development between Newport and Carisbrooke which took in the lower part of what is now Castle Road. Mrs Cook's house still stands, although with a later Victorian front, and from here Keats would have had a clear view to Carisbrooke Castle. This letter to his close friend John Hamilton Reynolds was written over two days.

Carisbrooke, April 17

My dear Reynolds – Ever since I wrote to my brothers in Southampton I have been in a taking – and at this moment I am about to be settled – for I have unpacked my books, put them in a snug corner, pinned up Haydon, Mary Queen of Scots and Milton with his daughters in a row. In the passage I found a head of Shakespeare which I had not seen before. It is most likely the same which George spoke so well of, for I like it extremely. Well – this head I have hung over my Books, just above the three in a row, having first discarded a French Ambassador – now this alone is a good morning's work. Yesterday I went to Shanklin which occasioned a great debate in my mind whether I should live there or at Carisbrooke. Shanklin is a beautiful place . . . Then why are you at Carisbrooke? say you. Because, in the first place, I should be at twice the Expense, and three time the inconvenience – next that from here I can see your continent – from a little hill close by the whole north Angle of the Isle of Wight, with the water between us. In the 3rd place I see Carisbrooke Castle from my window, and I have found several delightful wood-alleys, and copses, and quick freshes [streams]. As for primroses – the Island ought to be called Primrose Island – that is, if the nation of Cowslips agree thereto, of which there are divers Clans just beginning to lift up their heads. Another fixing is, that I am more in reach of the places around me. I intend to walk over the Island East – West – North – South. I have not seen many specimens of Ruins – I don't think however I shall see one to surpass Carisbrooke Castle. The trench is overgrown with smoothest turf, and the Walls with ivy. The Keep within side is one Bower of ivy – a colony of Jackdaws have been there for many years. I dare say I have seen many a descendant of some old cawer who peeped through the bars at Charles the first when he was there in confinement.

April 18th

. . . I find I cannot do without Poetry – without eternal Poetry – half the day will not do – the whole of it – I begin with little, but habit has made me a Leviathan. I had become all of a Tremble from not having written anything of late . . . I shall forthwith begin my Endymion, which I hope I shall have got some way with by the time you come, when we will read our verses in a delightful place I have set my heart upon, near the Castle. Give my love to your sisters severally – to George and Tom. Remember me to Rice, Mr. and Mrs. Dilke and all we know.

Your sincere Friend
John Keats

The Letters of John Keats, *Selected with an introduction by Hugh l'Anson Faucett*, (1938)

Endymion
Book I

A thing of beauty is a joy for ever:
Its loveliness increases; it will never
Pass into nothingness; but still will keep
A bower for us, and a sleep
Full of sweet dreams and health and quiet breathing.
Therefore, on every morrow, are we wreathing
A flowery band to bind us to the earth,
Spite of despondence, of the inhuman dearth
Of noble natures, of the gloomy days,
Of all the unhealthy and o'er darkened ways
Made for our searching; yes, in spite of all,
Some shape of beauty moves among the pall
From our dark spirits. Such the sun, the moon,
Trees old and young, sprouting a shady boon
For simple sheep; and such are daffodils
With the green world they live in; and clear rills
that for themselves a cooling covert make
'Gainst the hot season; the mid-forest brake,
Rich with a sprinkling of fair musk-rose blooms:
And such too is the grandeur of the dooms
We have imagined for the mighty dead;
All lovely tales that we have heard or read:
An endless fountain of immortal drink
Pouring unto us from the heaven's brink.

The Poems of John Keats

A Walking Tour of the Island 1826

In June 1826 two young men, J. and H. Oldershaw, walked round the Island commenting on what they saw in a lively account. They describe the Island in its infancy as a tourist resort.

Ventnor is a very small and retired place . . . It consists of a few cottages, a couple of inns, the hotel and the Crab and Lobster. At the last-named house we took up our quarters. The part allotted to visitors consists of two sitting-rooms and two bed-rooms, neatly furnished, and the host and hostess, by the name of Drudge, are well-behaved, clean, civil people.

From here, on the 29th of June, 1826, we started our walk, intending to reach Freshwater that night. A beautiful and romantic line of road brought us to the Sandrock Hotel. This is a very nice inn, beautifully situated in a fine picturesque part of the Island. It was the prettiest inn I think I ever saw. To those who have plenty of the needful I would recommend this place as a pleasant summer retreat; not that the charges here are more exorbitant than at other places of the sort in the Island. If any should ask me if the Isle of Wight were a cheap place for a holiday I should answer 'No', but where is the place that is at the same time cheap and fashionable? My dinner here cost me 36s (£1.80) without wine or ale, and, as for lodgings at Ventnor I could not find a bed and sitting room for less than a 'yellow-boy' (sovereign) a week. I have been to Windermere and Bangor and never gave more than 10s (50p) or half a guinea (55p) a week for lodgings.

Near the Sandrock Hotel is a spring which every stranger visits. The water contains salt, alum, and iron, and is said to be good for various complaints. The visitor may take a bottle of this precious water on payment of half a crown (12p), or he may drink a glass, but ten to one it makes him sick, as it tastes like ink.

The fine prospect from this down [Afton] we did not see, a thick fog coming on and continuing for the rest of the day. At length we came in sight of Freshwater Gate. The scenery here is fine and bold, the waves dashing with great violence against the perpendicular rocks, which rise to a great height.

From here we walked to Cowes, which is a gay, pleasant place in the season. Thither the fashionable resort, many of them having yachts of their own. Lord Yarborough has just had a remarkably fine yacht built, said to have cost £30,000, and he lives on board during the season. Cowes has a fine harbour, and the bathing is good. Lord Henry Seymour's marine castle [Norris] and Mr. Nash's castle [East Cowes] are both in view.

Ryde is a cheerful, gay town. It contains many pretty cottages. I should say for a summer residence it is full as pleasant a place as Cowes. There is a good inn and a noble pier which runs out many yards into the sea. Here also is good and commodious bathing with lots of machines (things I never enter myself; I would as soon think of crawling into a

Sedan). As we intended to reach Ventnor this night our stay was very short. We therefore walked through the town and on to Brading, and thence on to Shanklin through rather uninteresting country, except Sandown Bay, which is very fine.

This is a small, retired pleasant village enough, much frequented, sometimes by students from the universities. A party was there when we passed through. There are several good and comfortable lodging-houses and a rustic-looking inn, thatched and covered with ivy, as most of the cottages in the Island are. There is also a neat church, half a mile from the village, which appears to be rather a fashionable place. We went there one Sunday and saw many smart looking people. We then completed the circuit of the Island by walking back to Ventnor.

It must be allowed that the interior of the Island is very destitute of trees, there is little or no hedgerow timber, and in some parts it exhibits a rather dreary appearance, but the coast is well wooded in many parts and makes ample amends.

. . . to one meditating a tour of the Isle of Wight I would advise going from east to west, for this reason: The beauties will increase upon him as he goes and the best will be reserved to the last. All's well that ends well.'

Isle of Wight County Press, *Saturday May 4, (1929)*

A Gothic Undercliff

Mrs. Radcliffe, who wrote the splendid Gothic novel, The Mysteries of Udolpho *in 1794, visited the Island at the height of the romantic period and her comments on the Undercliff are what you might expect from such a writer.*

We entered upon it about a mile from Niton, and found ourselves in such a Druid scene of wildness and ruin as we never saw before. The road is, for the most part, close to the wall of rock, which seems to threaten the traveller with destruction, as he passes frequently beneath enormous masses that lean forward. On the other side of the road is an extremely rugged descent of about half-a-mile to the sea, where sometimes are amphitheatres of rocks, the theatres filled with ruins, and frequently covered with verdure and underwood that stretch up the hill-side with the wildest pomp, sheltering here a cottage, there a villa among the rocky hillocks. We afterwards ascended by a steep rugged road to the summit of the down, from which the views are astonishing and grand in a high degree; we seemed perched on an extreme point of the world, looking down on hills and cliffs of various height and form, tumbled into confusion as if by an earthquake, and stretching into the sea.

J. Redding Ware, The Isle of Wight, (*1875*)

A Summer Letter from Yarmouth

Today the SUN SHONE! I ought to write that in letters a foot high because the whole place is transformed, it was simply amazing. Everywhere was suddenly full of jolly people walking about with no shoes on, even in the shops. Mum was quite shocked, well, she thought it was all right in the ice-cream place, but the three-star hotel where we had our pub lunch was full of sandy feet too, and that really shook her. So perhaps it really does deserve to call itself the Holiday Island. Most of the sandy feet seemed to belong to the people who came off the yachts in Yarmouth Harbour - fancy having your own yacht! They must be stinking rich even if they can't afford shoes – hah hah! Yachts cost as much as motor cars, or even more, like thousands and thousands, but the harbour's full of them, it really is full, there's a notice up that says so, you can see it from the pier. And during the day they all go sailing out into the Solent, hundreds and hundreds of white sails, could be the Ml on water, but I daresay it's more fun than that. Can be quite hairy too because while we were having our pub lunch, very good sausage and chips, an enormous tanker came past, looking a bit like Jaws, and there's no way a ship that size could give way to all those sails even if it's supposed to, and then the ferry comes across and across, so perhaps it's a bit like dodgems and all that danger adds to the fun. There's a Castle next door to where we had lunch, but they agreed we had enough Culture yesterday so we were allowed NOT to visit it. They've got it on the list though for another rainy day. But it was so amazingly blissfully HOT that we were allowed to go swimming instead. Well, that is what we come on a seaside holiday for, isn't it? The sea was lovely but the beach was a bit pebbly and muddy and seaweedy. We came out with grey feet halfway up our legs like Wellingtons, it was really slimy – quite a nice feeling squelching through your toes . . .

Jill Chaney, Three Weeks in August, (*1995*)

4 · OLD TOWNS

Newport has survived as the main market town in the Island and was probably destined to be so from its foundation. A good tidal river which ensured connection with the mainland, the proximity of Carisbrooke Castle, the centre of royal administration, and despite periods of stagnation it has remained the centre of Island life.

Newport in Tudor Times

Newport, with a population in 1559 of 1175 in 240 houses, was by no means negligible in terms of contemporary town sizes. [It] lies in a hollow at a point where the valley of the Medina River slices through the east-west chalk ridge. Most of the town area is quite level, but the streets start dipping towards the river at the eastern end of the town, this contour feature and the bend of the river explaining the less regular pattern of the streets of this part of Newport. Basically the town comprises four main streets aligned south-west to north-east: Crocker Street, Lugley Street, High Street and Pyle Street, with their connecting cross streets. Such was the plan in 1559 and it is substantially unchanged today . . . Writing in 1633 Sir John Oglander observes: 'Since my Memory it was a very poore Towne the houses mostly Thatched, the streetes unpaved, and in the Hyghstrete where now be fayre Houses were

Garden Plottes'.

Newport never seems to have been a walled town, though the 16th-century terriers do indicate two main gates. One was the 'Towne Gate' at the foot of Hunnyhill on the road to Cowes; the other gate was at the Carisbrooke end of the town, a few yards from the junction of Pyle Street and High Street.

Of the public buildings in 1558 the central one was the 12th-century church of St. Thomas . . . In 1558 it was a chapel of ease to Carisbrooke, the town of Newport then lacking parochial status. Writing about Newport in the 1500s Sir John Oglander implies that the maintenance of the church was a heavy burden to the townspeople ; 'Mutch a Dooe they had to Patch up the Church, every Trade undertooke to Bwyld a Pece witnes on the walles the (signs) of the yarde And Taylors sheeres, and the horseshoe anvill, and hammor, etc.'

Then there was the town hall, the seat of civil government. At the point where Holyrood Street widened at its junction with High Street there was a little island of houses called the Falcon. In 1405-6 the bailiffs let a piece of waste ground just to the east of this for the building of two shops with a first floor solar for a new court house in which the bailiffs and commonality were to hold their courts. It became known as the Audit House. Some idea of its appearance may be retrieved from the inventory of its salvaged building at the time of demolition in 1838. These indicate that the roof was of 'slatts', the buildings of Flanders brick, and the interior was wood-panelled.

There were hardly any other public buildings in 1558. The harbour installations were as yet little developed, and the quay was muddy and unpaved. The archery butts were in one of the open spaces on the south side of South Street (then called Cosham Street); there was a market house in the main square, just opposite the west end of the church; there was a solitary alms house on the east side of Sea Street, near the quay; and there was a cattle pound at the western junction of High Street and Pyle Street, just inside the gate on the road to Carisbrooke.

Of the private houses and shops, some individual buildings can be distinguished. There was Chantry House on the south side of the eastern end of Pyle Street; and one or two named houses occupied by the more prosperous citizens. Hazards House, at the eastern end of the High Street on the north side was described in 1567 as 'late in the hands of Mr Porter' . . . Hazards House as it survived until 1968 had a 17th century brick façade but traces of the earlier merchants' cellar in the lower courses suggest a building of stone rather than brick. On the south side of South Street, next to the town butts, was a house called Coppid Hall, held by Robert Brackley who seems to have been the richest townsman of his day . . .

As for shops, those of the butchers were concentrated in a little row along the south side of the High Street to the north of the church . . . The fishmongers were close to them, and the whole area of this church square was regarded as the flesh shambles and market.

This then was the town in 1558: a compact saucer of low lying ground spreading south and west from the quay; as yet, only partly developed and with its buildings punctuated by gardens and meadows. It had a handful of more notable houses, in the hands of the prosperous merchants, but the town books suggest a large amount of rickety and poorly-maintained property. Oglander's scornful comment, written in 1631 that in the 16th century 'the stretes weare not paved, but laye most wett and Beasteley, with great stoppelles to stepp over the kennel from one syde to the other', does find some support in the town records.

Jack D. Jones, The Isle of Wight 1558-1642, (1978)

Princess Elizabeth's Tomb

Charles I's daughter Elizabeth spent three weeks in Carisbrooke Castle in 1650. She was a delicate child and when she was caught in the rain on the Bowling Green a simple chill became much more serious and she died on 8 September, aged almost fifteen years.

In the cold light of an autumn day in 1793 a number of workmen in the parish church at Newport began, under the instruction of the sexton, to prepare a grave for Mr Septimus Henry West. The place selected was in the Chancel near the altar, and after the stones of the paving had been removed and the first impressions made with picks and shovels the men were surprised to find themselves striking into a hitherto unknown vault.

Work was halted and a closer inspection made. When more fully revealed the vault proved to be lined with coarse uneven bricks, unplastered, and containing a plain lead coffin, across the widest part of which on brass strips was an inscription 'Elizabeth, 2nd daughter of ye late King Charles, Decd Sept 8th 1650.'

The finding of such a tomb caused quite a stir and the sexton without delay referred the whole matter to a higher authority. Accordingly Thomas Orde, Governor of the Island wrote . . . to the Rt. Hon. Henry Dundas . . . giving details of the finding of the vault . . . At the end of his letter he added . . . 'The coffin is perfect. It is my intention unless any other order be signified, to cause to be placed over the vault a large plain stone with a simple inscription in the manner of those of King Henry 6th and Edward 4th in the Cloisters of St. George's Chapel at Windsor.'

J.A. Viney, 'The tragic Princess' Wight Life, *June/July vol 12. No. 2*

Newport's New Church

The old church during seven centuries became very dilapidated, inside, the huge pews, the galleries and the arches made it impossible for many to see; the walls had become porous and let in the damp, and unless you were quite close to the East end you could not hear the service . . . it was decided to pull down the church and build a new one.

The foundation stone of the new church was laid on the 24th August, 1854, by the Prince Consort. The ancient pulpit (1636) and the alabaster monument to Sir Edward Horsey was retained in the new church . . . The Bishop Winchester consecrated the church on the 20th January, 1857.

When the present church was being erected Queen Victoria became aware of the fact that no monument had ever been put up to the memory of the Princess [Elizabeth]. Feeling that this was a reproach, the Queen commissioned Baron Marochetti, a famous Italian sculptor, and the magnificent monument which stands at the head of the North aisle was placed in the church.

At the same time the Queen and the Prince Consort commanded that windows on the North wall near the monument should be filled in with stained glass so that only a gentler light should fall on the tomb. The window above the monument is called 'The Maiden's Window', as it was subscribed for by the young ladies of Newport.

R.J. Eldridge, Newport Isle of Wight in Bygone Days, *(1952)*

Newtown

This was another, but later, medieval planned town, one of the six new
towns of the Bishop of Winchester. Using land on his estate, Swainston,
in or about 1256 the bishop granted a free borough and port to be laid
out on the edge of the creek. The town plan laid out two main streets in
an east-west alignment with cross streets running north-south. This plan
can still be traced, although the way now lies mostly in fields and grassy
lanes.

Today, Newtown is a little hamlet scattered between the arms of a creek,
pasture land, hazel copses and salt flats, on the way to nowhere; its only
large population the gulls, waders and geese out on the marsh, now
protected as a nature reserve: a green and peaceful corner of the Island
with little traffic even in high summer, and fascinating to explore on
foot.

From Shalfleet the lane crosses a narrow stone bridge over an arm of
the creek called Causeway Lake – to the west where it widens out stood
the old quays, long since disappeared, though the shapes still show up in
aerial photographs. A narrow channel winds away between the mud
flats, curlew crying in the distance; in winter flocks of black and white
lapwing fly in, while August purples the banks with sea lavender. Not a
house in sight. Walk on down the lane, though, and there is the town
hall, a sturdy brick building complete with balcony for announcing
election results, and open to the public in summer; the wide grassy space
on which it stands was part of Broad Street.

Just beyond lies one of the few old stone houses in Newtown, once the
village pub, with the coat of arms above its door. Here the tarmac lane
turns to the left into High Street, but look to the right also and there is
the eastern end of High Street continuing as a wide grass path . . .

Along High Street stand a few cottages, old and new, and the village
pump with a large iron wheel. This was the principal street of the town
as the name implies, and it still possible to see the lines of some of the
old burgage plots on either side where gardens or hedges still divide the
land into small parcels, though this was more evident before hundreds of
elms were lost in the epidemic of Dutch elm disease. At Woolgar's
cottage the lane swings right – it once continued straight on down to the
quay . . .

The lane turns another right angle out of Church Street into Gold

Street, though the eastern end is gold only with buttercups. A footpath leads down to the marsh where the grass banks of the old salt pans still enclose shallow water where tern dive for fish, though the salt house is now only a heap of bricks.

Round about 1700 the marsh to the east was reclaimed. This must have been an enormous undertaking, involving building a sea wall and sluices around 120 acres in a blunt triangle, all of which became pasture land. All this was changed by the great tide of 1954 which breached the wall and flooded the pasture, returning it to mud flats. Ever since the quarter mile of remaining sea wall has been a much-loved walk, but at the end of 1981 a tide as high as that of 1954 with a north-easterly gale behind it made a fresh breach, allowing the sea into the salt pans.'

Patricia Sibley, 'Newtown' The Island from Within – an Anthology, *(1983)*

The Newtown Rats

The legend of the Newtown rats emerged in the nineteenth century; an early prose account and in the 1860s the story in verse. Browning had written his famous poem of the 'Pied Piper of Hamelin' in 1842 and this may have stimulated local imagination to explain the decayed medieval town. There is no evidence that this was an old legend; Sir John Oglander in the early seventeenth century comments on the Hamelin story and he would have been aware of a similar local legend, but none is mentioned. The story in verse uses the legend to explain why Francheville [Newtown] was unprepared for the French raid in 1377.

Twas in the reign of Edward Three,
    The King was waging Northern wars,
And left the country south of Dee
    A prey to rapine, feuds and jars . . .

From what is said you'll understand
    The Island being in disorder;
The vermin got the upper hand,
    And Rats o'er ran the farmers border.

In milkpans, in the brewing vats,
    In corn-bins, in the children's beds –

Everywhere the wretched Rats
    With their long tails and filthy heads.

At last the magistrates decreed,
    A guerdon of one hundred pounds
To him who should have fully freed
    From pestilential rats their bounds.

A hundred pounds was then no song,
    But none adventured, all were dumb;
A wandering piper came along
    Who said he'd do it for the sum. . . .

To kill the rats and guard the grain,
    No weapon had he save his flute,
Preluding with a merry strain,
    He left the mayor with low salute.

Now singly, now by threes and fours,
    By tens and twenties ten times told,
From windows, cellars, roofs and doors
    Pour'd forth the rats – one hideous fold! . . .

Still pouring floods of harmony
    The Piper there his craft unbound;
And following after him to sea,
    The music loving Rats were drowned.

In Franchville streets then folks were glad,
    Again the Farmer breathed at ease,
Felt owner of what crops he had,
    And housed his corn, and beans and peas. . . .

So as the seasons went and came,
    Men forgot Piper, Rats and all,
Till one day, in bright rags, his claim
    Standing he urged in the Town Hall.

The magistrates declared was jest
    To give for sing-song such a boon,
But threw some ducats from the chest,
    And bade him go and play a tune.

The Piper did as he was told,
    He went away and played his Flute
But turned his back upon the gold,
    And left the Mayor without salute.

Whilst inland, every path you take
    Stand listeners, eloquently mute;
But most the children seem awake
    To the strange magic of that flute.

And now the sacrifice is over;
    One splash, and Ocean's curling wreath
Is all the fond eye can discover,
    The Children calmly sleep beneath.

Ah! then was wailing deep and loud
    In Francheville streets, where all was blight,
The strong man to the dust is bowed
    And the young matron's hair is white . . .

Still as the seasons went and came,
    Men rallied somewhat and awoke,
But Francheville never was the same
    That it had been before the stroke.

Beata Elizabeth Macauly, An Isle of Wight Legend, (*1869*)

5 · NEW TOWNS

Cowes

Cowes is a town that has evolved from a few warehouses and small boat yards, adapting itself to the times until it burst into fashionable life in the nineteenth century when yachting in the grand manner came on the scene. Sir John Oglander in the early seventeenth century begins the story.

The Birth of Cowes

I knew when there were not above 3 or 4 houses at Cowes, and I was, and am, persuaded that if our wars and troubles had not unfortunately happened, it would have grown as famous as Newport. For it was much approved by all the eastern parts of the world as a fit place for them to victual in . . . where I have seen 300 ships at anchor. And, if the country had but had so much discretion as to make good use of that harbour as, first to build store-houses, to have a magazine for all provisions, and to deal with the Dutch so they would victual there, they need no other market or means to make the island happy and fortunate.

F. *Bamford,* A Royalists Notebook (*1936*)

Observations on the Commerce of Cowes – 1801

Cowes, where the Custom-house is situated, affords a very convenient and commodious harbour; foreign ships, both on their outward and homeward bound voyages, frequently resort thither for shelter from adverse winds, or to repair damages sustained in tempestuous gales. Vessels bound to the Northern parts of Europe often in the winter season stop here for several months, waiting the opening of the navigation of their frozen rivers; and a great number of American ships also stop here for orders to what markets to proceed, which are generally lodged with the American Consul resident there, previous to their arrival.

Cowes is one of the ports allotted for the warehousing of foreign corn and rice, and it is also one of the ports, and the only one in the Channel between Falmouth and London, at which the importation and warehousing of tobacco and snuff is by law allowed.

The convenient quays and wharfs for shipping, and the commodious stores on each side of the harbour, offer opportunities for a much greater and more extended import and export trade at this port than of late years has fallen to its share.

Hampshire Repository vol. II (*1801*)

Cowes Week 1870

Cowes in 1870 differed little in essentials from the Cowes of half a century earlier. It was rendered easier of access by an improved steamboat service and by railways and telegraphs, but it retained all its old features of an interesting, if inconvenient, fishing village shut in between the sea and the Northwood estate, and altogether innocent of most of the attractions of an ordinary seaside resort. Bathing machines were rarities, nigger minstrels unknown, and the glories of the Parade were yet to come. In its High Street then as now, if two carriages met the wheels of one went over the pavement and the foot passengers took refuge in the shops for safety. There was an interesting fusion of trades in those shops, which doubtless had its convenience, where you get cigars at the chemist, poultry at the greengrocer's, and herrings and pigs' heads with bleeding noses from the hooks where they hung in rows on the shop fronts of the ironmongers. It was reckoned a great day in

Cowes when in that happy year 1870 a hairdresser first established himself as a permanency and the itinerant artist from Newport, who had previously shorn the locks of the community at proper intervals, found his occupation gone. Cowes tradesmen, in fact, little realised the greatness which was shortly to be thrust upon them, or dreamed that the fashion which was shortly to fill their modest lodgings would decree that no jacket for man or skirt for woman who peopled its yachts and its streets during the annual gathering, be deemed of true fashionable cut unless it had its origin in one or two modest establishments in the little High Street.

There are many vivid pictures of the aspect of Cowes of thirty years ago preserved . . .

'Nothing like its aspect,' says one [visitor] 'was ever seen out of a box of Dutch toys. From the sea it looks like a heap of superior dog-kennels which have been rolled down the hill on which it lies and brought up full on the edge of the water; the in-and-outness of its waterside premises seem incredible, and the rooms of its houses on shore are built on the model of yacht cabins which is the highest flight of the Cowes imagination. Longing eyes have been cast by many an agent on the Ward estate, which happily closes in the houses between itself and the sea, and every kind of plan has been made for cutting it up into desirable villas of the cockney type.'

Cowes, however, has been preserved from the worst evils of what is called 'improvement' at most seaside places, and still presents many of the features which struck the writers thirty years ago. Fashion was then content to make the most of its modest accommodation during the few weeks which it devoted to the pleasures of the place. Fashion has really continued in much the same mood since, and is satisfied with accommodation in Cowes in August which it would reject with derision elsewhere. The town has a charm of its own apart from the social attractions of the gatherings which have given it its modern vogue . . .

The society was the same year after year. 'The same party crowded into the same little houses and filled the same villas, the same wicker chairs were set out in the club lawn and filled with identical people who had been pillars of the little town for years. Here they greeted each other almost like relations; here they are kindly, considerate, almost affectionate, and the outsider feels almost like an intruder upon a family party. They all know each other's little histories and secrets, and their conversations bristle with little allusions, the unintelligibility of which to all outside intelligence makes a high and inseparable barrier to all intercourse of the same kind.

Montague Guest and William B. Boulton, Memorials of the Royal Yacht Squadron, *(1902)*

Winning in Cowes Week

The social events in Cowes Week are the trimmings – the real work of the Week is winning races. Uffa Fox, the ebullient boat builder and yachtsman tells how he did this in 1967.

The Royal Yacht Squadron, the best club in the world, welcomes seven of the important clubs to use its clubhouse and line for the Week; this makes the organisation simple as each and every class starts over the same line at the same time on each of the 'nine-days wonder' that is Cowes Week.

. . . Prince Philip owns *Coweslip*, No. 192 in the [Flying Fifteen] class; . . . when Prince Philip or Prince Charles cannot use her I have had this privilege. So it came to pass that, in my seventieth year, I raced her on the Royal Thames Yacht Club's day of Cowes Week 1967.

The first race of the day starts at 10.30 and different classes go off at ten minute intervals until 1 p.m., so although it is best to start to the westward against the prevailing wind, it is more important that in calm and light airs the classes are swept off the line on their way round the course by the tide, otherwise the line could be cluttered up with hundreds of racers, in utter confusion, unable to make their headway against the tide. On this occasion the day's breeze had not filled for the early races so all classes started down tide to the eastward. We, in the Flying Fifteens were fortunate in starting two hours ten minutes after the first race as by then we had a brave breeze from the south-west; all that we could endure without reefing.

The Isle of Wight is diamond in shape and the prevailing south-west wind drives true up the Solent from the Needles to Cowes but there the Island is cut in two, north and south by the River Medina, and this same wind funnels from the south out of this river. The majority of yachtsmen do not realise this, as often the Solent south-wester over-rides the southerly from the river.

There were thirty in our class, all darting about like swifts and as we wanted to manoeuvre as we wished in the first half-mile, my crew, the late Geoffrey Budden, and I decided it was better to be able to do so than set the spinnaker and be captive to it in spite of the higher speed this great, ballooning sail gives.

The Seaview Mermaid's starting cannon was our ten-minute signal and when our starting flags were hauled down away we dashed, most of our fleet flying spinnakers and for the first 50 yards these forged ahead but then the strong southerly out of the river put them aback and, while they were busy gathering their big sails in and losing speed, we pulled up and were in the first six. Now with river wind eliminated we set our spinnaker and were soon swishing swiftly eastward in complete control, quite content to be bunched closely in the first half-dozen boats so soon in the race because one of us was certain to win; we were so far ahead of the other twenty- four competitors.

More than twenty years earlier I had over-strained my heart designing and developing the airborne lifeboats that saved many a gallant airman's life, for when we are saving lives we cannot count the cost. Ever since then I had to race with the burden of this, so we took things as gently as we could without losing any places.

We successfully gybed round the Eastern Mark, after taking in and stowing our spinnaker, and settled down to a planing reach to the South Bramble Buoy against the flood tide, all of us keeping our positions.

After rounding that we faced up to the hardest part of the race, a dead beat to windward against a strong south-wester and the flood tide, with heavy spray flying right over us, to the east of Gurnard Buoy, through the line for the second round, to gybe round the Eastern Mark again and on the high planing reach to the South Bramble Buoy.

It was now or never, to win we must pass the first boat on this hard beat to windward and it was for this effort I had saved my heart from hard work and now it had its strength stored enough to stand the pressure. Slowly and surely we worked our way out to windward and finally rounded the East Gurnard with a quarter of a mile lead.

Geoff set the spinnaker swiftly and with a fair wind and tide we soon sailed to the music of the winning cannon across the finish line, by a quarter of a mile. *Coweslip* had won the Royal Thames Yacht Club's Holt Cup for the sixth time.

Uffa Fox, More Joys of Living, *(1972)*

America's Cup Jubilee Regatta

The best ball ever.

2,200 guests, feeling more privileged than usual, made their way to the attending motor launches with a sense of excitement and high expectation. Crowds of onlookers lined the promenade, and the walk down the jetty seemed more like the red carpet to a film premiere. As guests nonchalantly waited for the water taxis, the shimmer of gilt and glitter sparkled in the setting sun. In fact, there were so many exquisite women in Valentino and Armani that the rules changed. Impossible to outdo each other by designer label, points could only be scored if their escort had the most braid on his jacket (double marks for Royal insignia).

At Osborne House roller-skating guides and a living 'statue' of Queen Victoria welcomed the party goers. After strolling through the property's elegant hallways, one is normally met by a magnificent view over the Solent. The impression on arriving this time, however, was not the vast lawns sweeping down to the sea but the vast sea of glamorous people swarming the terraces. As guests mingled above the manicured, illuminated gardens, Moët et Chandon bubbled merrily into glasses, canapés melted into mouths and the Band of Her Majesty's Royal Marines beat the Retreat. Glancing round, you could see this ball was like no other. In one corner the Aga Khan and his wife Princess Gabriella chatted merrily to HRM Juan Carlos de Borbon. In another, the Aspreys daintily pushed past Bill Koch, while Robin Aisher vied for a waiter's attention with Susan Sangster.

Dinner was another remarkable affair. Picture the largest marquee imaginable, then add a north-wing extension. It was so huge, it took, on average, 20 minutes to locate the right table. Not that anyone complained. It was rather amusing asking the way of passing royalty, sailing personalities, models, aristocracy and the general rich and famous. Likewise, conversation blossomed in the buffet queue, where you were never quite sure if you were passing over the salad spoons to a billionaire or a waiter in a black tie . . .

Soon after dinner, dancing became more and more abandoned. As the disco classics pounded out, beautifully coiffed hairstyles dismantled into rock chic, bow ties left necks to swing wildly about the head, and no toe was safe from a Jimmy Choo stiletto . . .

Finally, at 1 a.m., the call for last boats home echoed through the marquee. As laughing couples drifted across the grass, dinner jackets draped on female shoulders, military caps at drunken angles, there was only one complaint to be heard. The Cinderella ball had ended far, far, too soon. On the other hand, everyone knew there was a race tomorrow, and nobody loves a tired old pumpkin. It was time for the pooped to hit the deck.

Kit Hob, The Official Book, The America's Cup Jubilee 2001, (2002)

East Cowes

In the early nineteenth century East Cowes was regarded as an adjunct to Cowes, a rural landscape with two handsome castles. The first, Norris Castle, was built by Lord Henry Seymour, and it was a story about this elderly gentleman that intrigued a visitor in 1826, when he wrote it up in his journal.

By all accounts his lordship is a most eccentric character. They say he has not been out of the Island for 20 or 30 years. He is an old bachelor, lives very retired and from his dress, which generally consists of a blue jacket and trousers and hob-nailed boots, you would not know him from a labourer, for which he has been more than once taken. He works with his men hedging and ditching, and has been known to ride into Cowes on a dung cart, and even go to a ball in it. The story is told that a gentleman walking in his grounds met a man whom he presumed to be a labourer, but was, in fact Lord Seymour himself. The stranger conducted over the grounds by the 'labourer' was highly delighted, and called Lord Henry a man of exquisite taste and such like, in which the 'labourer' acquiesced. Upon approaching the house the 'labourer' invited the stranger in and orders him a meal in the servants' hall. They then separate, the stranger to enjoy his repast and his lordship his little joke.

His lordship has more than once played the part of a labourer in so conducting visitors over the grounds. He has even accepted money from them, and on his return to the house has given it to the servants with the remark: 'Here you are! I've got something for you today.'

Isle of Wight County Press, *Saturday May 4* (1929)

A Visit to East Cowes Castle

John Nash was building East Cowes Castle just about the same time as Lord Henry Seymour was building Norris, but Nash was a very different character, outgoing and sociable. He too welcomed visitors, who could see the interior of his castle – even when the family was at home, as Joseph Farington found in 1817.

. . . on a fine September morning [he] presented his card at the large lodge and was told that he and his party might see the house and grounds . . . Entering at the porch . . . the Faringtons passed down a short corridor to the rather dull lop-sided vestibule and thence to the staircase tower . . . From here the servant 'very civilly showed us the dining room, in which a table was genteely set for dinner for seven persons.' This room was ornamented with several pictures - views of houses designed by Mr Nash. 'The servant then told us', continued Farington, 'we might pass through the opposite room, the drawing room, in which was Mr Nash with company, all of whom were seated when we entered, and we only passed through the middle of the room to the conservatory. Mr Nash bowed . . . ' At this stage Farington presented the servant with two shillings, 'with which he appeared pleased.'

Ian Sherfield, East Cowes Castle, The Seat of John Nash, Esq. A Pictorial History, (1994)

Mary Toms – A Woman Preacher

The Bible Christians, an off-shoot of the Weslyan Methodists, were founded in 1815 by William Bryan. Their mission field was mainly among the poorest rural labourers and they were unusual in encouraging women to take an active part in preaching the written word of the Bible, the foundation of their movement. When Mary Toms from Cornwall arrived in the Island in 1823 she was to be a local wonder.

Tuesday July 29th (1823) Mary Toms sailed from Plymouth for the Isle of Wight and arrived at West Cowes at ten o'clock at night. There was no one to meet her, and there was not a person in the place whom she knew. It was with considerable difficulty that she secured a place to sleep

for the night, and when she did, it would appear that the Lord had most
to do with it. The place was very full of people it being regatta week. The
person who at last took her in was Mrs. Pooke, the wife of a shoemaker.
They were Wesleyans. The following Sunday she went to East Cowes for
the purpose of preaching in the open air, – alone, without a single person
on whom she could rely for help. The weather was most inclement –
wind and rain – but having obtained the loan of a chair, on which to
stand to deliver her message, she commenced to sing –

> Come ye sinners, poor and wretched,
> Weak and wounded, sick and sore;
> Jesus ready stands to save you,
> Full of pity, joined with power;
> He is able,
> He is willing, doubt no more.

Numbers of persons gathered round the young woman to hear what she
had to say. There was a novelty about it and the service caused much
interest and excitement . . . The young evangelist announced that (D.V.)
she would conduct another service on the morrow in the open air should
the weather be favourable, and should it not be, the service should be
under shelter. A woman . . . offered a room in her house. This offer was
accepted, but when the time came the crowd was so large to hear this
'woman preacher' that all the rooms in the house were not sufficient to
accommodate the multitude. The only alternative, therefore, was again
to preach in the open air . . . there was also present at that service a lady
and gentleman who had been too proud ever to hear a dissenting brother
preach, but went out of curiosity to hear this dissenting sister, and were
so impressed with what they heard, that many times after that they
greatly befriended her. It was quite striking in those days to see a lady
with fine ribbons and long waving feathers, attend the preaching of, and
standing by the person of a 'Bryanite' evangelist . . . Mary Toms soon
had more invitations to preach in other parts of the Island than she could
accept.

Rev. J. Woolcock, A History of the Bible Christian Churches in the Isle of Wight,
(1897)

Ryde

Ryde officially came into being with the passage of the Ryde Improvement Act 1829 when it was recognized as a town taken out of the parish of Newchurch. It was the first nineteenth century town and soon established itself as a fashionable seaside resort for the wealthy. In its earlier existence as Upper and Lower Ryde, two small villages, it did receive visitors, although their arrival could be hazardous as Henry Fielding found on his brief stay in 1754. He was in extreme poor health, suffering from dropsy, but he still managed a light-hearted account of his eccentric landlady at the Old Nag's Head in Upper Ryde.

Saturday, July 13. I was persuaded by my wife to go ashore and stay at Ryde until we sailed. I was pretty easily conveyed on board [a large hoy], but to get from thence to the shore was not so easy a task . . .

In fact, between the sea and the shore, there was, at low water, an impassable gulph, if I may so call it, of deep mud, which could neither be traversed by walking nor by swimming, so that for nearly one half of the twenty-four hours, Ryde was inaccessible by friend or foe . . .

I was at last hoisted into a small boat, and being rowed pretty near the shore, was taken up by two sailors, who waded with me through the mud, and placed me in a chair on the land, whence they afterwards conveyed me a quarter of a mile further to a house, which seemed to bid the fairest for hospitality in Ryde.

Mrs Humphreys no sooner received the news of our intended arrival, than she considered more the gentility than the humanity of her guests, and forgetting to put on her pot, fell to washing her house

[My wife] had found, tho' not under the same roof, a very snug apartment belonging to Mr Humphreys, and which had escaped the mop, by his wife being satisfied it could not possibly be visited by gentlefolk.

This was a dry, warm, oaken floored barn, lined on both sides with wheaten straw, and opened at one end into a green field, and a beautiful prospect. Here, without hesitation, she ordered the cloth to be laid, and came hastily to snatch me from worse peril by water than the common dangers of the sea. At length we were seated in one of the most pleasant spots, I believe, in the kingdom, and were regaled with our beans and bacon. We now waited with impatience for the arrival of our second course, which necessity and not luxury had dictated. This was a joint of mutton which Mrs Humphrys had been ordered to provide; but when, being tired with expectation, we ordered our servants *see for something else*, we were informed that there was nothing else; on which Mrs Humphrys being summoned, declared there was no such thing as mutton to be had in Ryde.

When I expressed my astonishment at there having no butcher in a village so situated, she answered that they had a very good one, and one that killed all sorts of meat in season, beef two or three times a year, and mutton the whole year round; but that it being then beans and pease time, he killed no meat, by reason he was sure of not selling it.

This she had not thought worthy of communication, any more than that there lived a fisherman next door, who was then provided with plenty of soals, and whitings, and lobsters, far superior to those which adorn a city feast. This discovery being made by accident, we completed the best, the pleasantest, and the merriest meal, with more appetite, more real, solid, luxury and more festivity, than was ever seen in an entertainment at White's.

Henry Fielding, Ed. Austin Dobson, Journal of a Voyage to Lisbon 1755, *(1907)*

Lodgings

Nine-tenths of the private house in Ryde are lodging houses, and the tourist who sojourns here for a few days or weeks, has an ample field before him for selection. Boards attached to the fronts, or suspended in the windows, will direct him in his search, or he may apply to any of the house agents, of whom the principal are, Messrs. Wallis, Marvin, Riddett, Scott and James , in Union Street, and Mr Knight in Pier Street.

Ryde is essentially a summer resort, and it is deservedly a great favourite with those who visit it at that time; and consequently the charges are the highest. In the winter there is a considerable reduction, and you may obtain first rate houses for a smaller sum than in the height of the season you would pay for a very second-rate lodging.

Rev. Edmund Venables, A Guide to the Isle of Wight, *(1860)*

Ryde Pier

The Isle of Wight had been ahead even of Brighton with the original Ryde Pier, whose first stone was laid on 29 June 1813 – a momentous day in the history of piers. The perilous embarkation and disembarkation of seafaring visitors became a thing of the past: thanks to the new pier, they could get on and off boats in relative safety and comfort. But Ryde Pier at that time was little more than a twelve-foot-wide wooden jetty for the use of small sailing craft. As the size of ships increased, so did the pier. Throughout the century it was extended and altered, eventually reaching a length of half a mile. By the 1860s it had been lengthened and widened to accommodate not only larger ships but a pier tramway, and in 1880 a railway was built alongside the pier; it is still in operation. Ryde thus became a three-purpose pier with accommodation for pedestrians and cars, the tramway and the railway.'
Cyril Bainbridge, Pavilions on the Sea, A History of the Seaside Pleasure Pier, *(1986)*

Ryde Pier and Pavilion 1951

You must picture a gigantic octagonal-shaped structure with walls of yellow slatted wood, serried windows picked out in green and a dome that seemed to be made of overlapping fish-scales. Attached to its right flank are two identical smaller domes, set side by side like a salt and pepper cruet. Flowing out from between these is a sun-deck, fenced with fancy green iron railings, that forms the roof of the pier-head tram station.

Picture a July morning in 1951 . . . with the sky around the fish-scale dome a deep cloudless blue and the sun shining as it only ever does in remembered childhood. The tide is at its highest, a weed-skeined grape-greenness, heaving and sploshing only a foot or two below the pier-head's concrete platform. Ryde is a far-off mirage of perpendicular hills, pale ice-cream colours and beaches on which hardly a square foot of sand remains unoccupied . . .

This is the last great age of the railway 'cheap day' excursion ticket and of the seaside day tripper. Every few minutes, the trains pull into Portsmouth Harbour station, crammed with city dwellers agog for however fleeting a taste of the Island's Riviera atmosphere. From

'Pompey', as the sailors have known Portsmouth since Nelson's time, there is a further half-hour's journey across six choppy miles of water between the nearest of the two seaborne forts to Ryde Pier-head. The black and white yellow-funnelled ferries – some modern steamships, some antiquated 'paddlers' – ply virtually non-stop on their diagonal course. More often than not they approach the pier-head with their eager passengers all crowded on the disembarkation side, making the deck heel over almost to the waterline,

As the crowds struggle down the narrow gangways, three voices booming over loudspeakers from widely separate quarters greet them with a bewildering diversity of information, exhortation and advice.

Voice number one comes from the pier-head railway station, from which steam trains pulling scarlet carriages with running boards connect with the Island's west coast resorts. The voice belongs to a British Railway official known as Taffy, a portly Welshman who wears his black serge uniform with the swagger of a Napleonic hussar and rolls his r's like a bard declaiming poetry. 'Good morning, ladies and gentlemen, good morning. This is Rrryde Pier – Rrryde Pier head. Upon disembarking, Rrryde passengers go to the rright after you pass the gate and straight down the pier on the trram. Trrain passengers to the left for services to Rrryde Esplanade, Rrryde St. Johns, Brrading, Sandown, Shanklin, Wrroxall and Ventnor . . .

Voice number two comes from a wooden hut with a striped awning situated next to the ticket-barrier for Ryde-bound holiday makers. This the pier-head rock shop, operated by my father's arch-enemy, Alfie Vernon. Mr Vernon himself has the microphone and is speaking in his usual damnably light, fluent and persuasive tone; 'Hello there, ladies and gentlemen, just across here at the shop, you've got plenty of time, we'll serve you straight away. We've got bars of chocolates, boiled sweets and toffees as well as rock in three flavours, peppermint, greengage or pineapple . . .'

Voice number three issues from two pairs of square-mouthed loudspeakers, mounted on the Pavilion's seaward-facing perimeter, and belongs to my father; 'Morning coffee and biscuits, tea, minerals and light refreshments are now being served on the sun-roof or in the restaurant upstairs. The entrance is on the tramway station. There is no queuing and no waiting. Make certain of your meal in comfort before you leave the pier . . .

Philip Norman, Babycham Night, (2003)

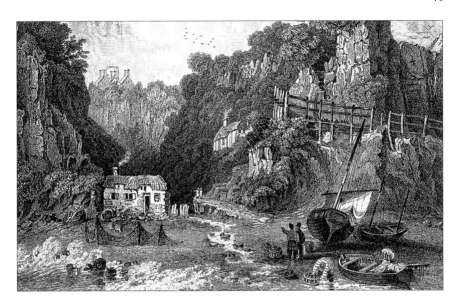

6 · SANDOWN, SHANKLIN AND VENTNOR

These three towns developed over a period of a hundred years. Shanklin was the first to attract visitors, as its dramatic scenery exactly suited the mood of the time. Ventnor grew rapidly from the 1840s as a winter resort whose soft airs made it suitable for invalids suffering from chest complaints. Sandown had to wait until later in the century, when the railway brought thousands to enjoy its wide sands and safe bathing.

Shanklin

Shanklin has no ancient lineage; or rather, though the land has been owned and cultivated time out of mind, the village was too insignificant as well as too remote to have left anything but the scantiest records. Insignificant, that is, until the latter half of the 18th century when Englishmen began increasingly to explore the remoter and wilder parts of their own country which, for the first time, they were coming to appreciate. It was in fact the opening of the Romantic Age in art, music, and literature which lay behind this new taste for mountains, lakes and coasts. Hence the attraction of the Isle of Wight among other places for the generation of 1770-1790. It is they who may be said to have 'discovered' the Isle of Wight, they who rhapsodized about its 'picturesque', 'sublime' and romantic scenery. Shanklin, and above all Shanklin Chine were high among the places they admired and eulogized. Before long the first visitors were followed by the first non-native residents, and they in turn were followed by visitors in vastly increased numbers as the railways made the Island accessible and the Victorian seaside holiday made it desirable . . . [transforming] the sleepy village about 1860 into the smart affluent, and beautiful Victorian watering place.

The Chine

From about 1770 . . . travellers visited the Chine . . . to admire the dramatic ravine (then much wilder and far less easy of access than now) which suited their notions of sublime and romantic scenery to perfection . . . Fisherman's Cottage, as it later became known, was built by William Colenutt at the foot of the chine at some time between his leasing the land in 1817, and 1824 . . . The owner of Fisherman's Cottage undertook to maintain the path through the Chine in return for which the lady of the manor allowed him to be the sole guide without whom no stranger gained admission.

John Keats 1817 and 1819

Shanklin is a most beautiful place . . . Our window looks over house tops and Cliffs to the Sea, so that when the Ships sail past the Cottage chimneys you may take them for weathercock. We have Hill and Dale, Forest and Mead and plenty of lobsters –

Gerard Manley Hopkins 1863

Shanklin is a delightful place . . . The sea is beautifully coloured and always calm, bathing delightful, sketches charming, walking tours and excursions, poetic downs, the lovely Chine, fine cliffs, everything (except odious Fashionables) –

Lindsay Boynton, Georgian and Victorian Shanklin – a pictorial history, (1973)

Sandown

When the nineteenth century poet Algernon Swinburne left Eton he was attracted to entering the army, but his family refused absolutely to consider this. Shortly afterwards he was walking along the shore near Culver Cliff and considering whether his idea of bravery would hold in a practical situation. On the spur of the moment he decided to climb it to test his nerve. He wrote his account of the adventure to his cousin, Mrs. Disney Leith.

It wasn't so hard as it looked, most of the way, for a light weight and a sure foot and a good steady head; but as soon as I got near the top I remember thinking that I should not like to climb down again. In a minute or two I found that I must, as the top part of the precipice came jutting out aslant of me for some feet . . . So of course I felt I must not stop to think for one second, and began climbing, hand under hand, as fast and steadily as I could, till I reached the bottom, and . . . began to look for another possible ascent at the same height . . . I was most of the way up again when I heard a sudden loud sound as of loud music . . . I glanced aside, and saw the opening of a great hollow in the upper cliff, out of which came a swarming of [seagulls] . . . They rose all about me in a heaving cloud – and then scattered.

. . . I was a little higher, quite near the top or well within hail of it, when I thought how queer it would be if some scanty foothold gave way; and at that very minute it did(I assure you on my word of honour that this is the exact truth, strange as it sounds and is} and I swung in the air by my hands from a ledge on the cliff which just gave room for the fingers to cling and hold on. There was a projection of rock to the left at which I flung out my feet sideways and just reached it; this enabled me to get breath and crawl at full speed (so to say) up the remaining bit of cliff. At the top I had not strength left to turn or stir; I lay down on my right side helpless . . . when I became unconscious . . . On returning to conscious life I found a sheep's nose just over mine and the poor good fellow-creature's eyes gazing into my face with a look of such kindly pity and sympathy as well as surprise . . . I couldn't help bursting into such a shout of laughter . . . that the sheep scuttled off.

Mrs Disney Leith, The Boyhood of Algernon Charles Swinburne, (1917)

A Seaside Home at Sandown

Maud Tomlinson was twenty three when she and her parents came to live at Sandown. Maud's life in the Island was commonplace, but for this reason her description of small-town middle class life has its own charm as we share with her the local events in Sandown in the 1880s.

August 1889

Dined at Major Remington's to meet his niece, a vicar's daughter from Brampton. Discussed the rival attractions of Sandown and Shanklin, to both of which she is new. Strange to say, she did not seem to be impressed by either, and said she would be glad to get back to Cumberland.

A hurricane blew all day today. Sea-fog and rain whirled about us as we set off, mackintoshes and galoshes, for the naval Review at Stokes Bay. Had a robust lunch, with roast beef and a galantine of chicken, before we discovered the Naval Review had been postponed. Went round the Fleet in a steam-launch, instead, which was the greatest of fun. I found a dry, warm and comfortable seat on the boiler with the chimney as a back. Immensely enjoyable day, and a great treat to see our brave sailors in such spirits.

Colonel Berkeley is here on holiday . . . Colonel Berkeley is such a distinguished man. He still seems to feel the death of his wife very badly . . . his face seems set in impenetrable gloom. He is such a fine looking man, it seems a great shame. Lilian and I have invited Colonel Berkeley to share with us a picnic at Whitecliff Bay. Wondered if our invitation is quite proper, but Lilian quelled my doubts. Could not sleep last night for worrying. Would a soldier of Colonel Berkeley's distinction care to bivouac on the downs with us?

It all passed relatively well. Colonel Berkeley does have the most distinguished manners. He refused to take the last Scotch egg. Possibly he might have seen that Lilian was eyeing it hungrily. And, thank heavens, he brought his own bottle of stout. As we had forgotten the sandwiches, we were suitably grateful when, on our return to Sandown, the Colonel bought us all tea and scrumptious scones at Agatha's tea rooms. Such a lively sense of humour. He said he had had more to eat when on duty in the Kashmir hills. Think he was joking. He bought us both boxes of chocolates to end a perfect day.

Three and a half years later the outcome of this first picnic was celebrated.

The County Press reported – 'On Thursday afternoon, at Christchurch, the marriage of Miss Tomlinson, of this place, with Colonel James Cavan Berkeley, of St. James's, London was celebrated in the presence of only a few spectators, owing to the success with which the date of the ceremony was kept secret.

Maud's diary naturally gave a full account of the great day. Her parents did not attend . . . but her father gave her a set of Milton and her mother a comb-case, 'to mark my nuptials'.

Never really thought I would be first, of Lilian and me, to grace the altar of Christchurch in a wedding veil. This Thursday 21st January, I waited, with Mr. Boucher at my side, for dear Jim to come up the aisle. I wore heavy silk poplin lined with crisp taffeta, and I got Mrs Gibbon to tag silver flounces all round the hem and neckline to the great advantage of the dress. I carried white chrysanthemums and my hat was trimmed with some birds' feathers. I really looked my best for Jim.

It was very quiet, and Jim and I exchanged our vows very simply and solemnly. Could not help but be glad that none of Jim's daughters had come. We would have looked very strange, a bride of thirty two and daughters not much younger. We had tremendous fun in the vestry . . . Everyone insisted on coming in. We had difficulty in getting the register signed at all, especially as Shoggie [Boucher] suddenly had the bright idea of hiding it from view, which confused all considerably.

Jim has decided on Ventnor as a suitable place for our honeymoon. We go for a great many constitutionals, though the weather is unremittingly bad. . . . Returned to Sandown. The Great G [her father] and I had a tearful farewell in the library. He pressed a copy of Keat's poems on me, saying that, now I was a married lady, it was suitable for me to read such verses. Feel most touched by his thoughtfulness.

Flora Fraser, Maud, the Diaries of Maud Berkeley, *(1985)*

Sandown 1916

Sandown began its independent existence in 1847, having been formerly part of the parish of Brading. The town is therefore quite modern, and is being developed on up-to-date lines.

. . . at Sandown it is rather hard to get away from [the] subject of bathing. It is the pride and glory of the place. The slope of the shore is so gradual that there is absolutely no danger, and there are no rocks or shingle to trouble the tender-footed. The bathing machines, too, are neater in appearance and better cared for than is the case at most resorts. The boating at Sandown is also excellent, and even such frail crafts as canoes can be navigated in perfect safety. When the tide is out, the sands are generally crowded with children, paddling, and castle-building or listening delightedly to the pierrots and other entertainers. Sandown is *par excellence*, the children's playground.

Ward, Locke & Co Ltd, (1916)

Ventnor

Ventnor grew from a tiny fishing community into a nationally known area where sufferers from chest diseases could safely remain during the winter. It was included in Spas of England *by Dr. Granville in 1841 and gives an accurate description of the situation at that time. A visitor who had spent the winter there provided the information.*

I can have no objection to giving you my impressions with regard to this place, Ventnor, as the task of describing its perfections will not occupy much time, for as yet it has not many except its climate. Having been here since November last, I can in that respect assure that it was *exquisite*, compared with any other place at which I have spent a winter . . .

Although the winter we have gone through was such a one as has not been known here before, the thermometer was never below 20 degrees out of doors, and that only during two or three nights. The state of vegetation is the strongest test of its mildness, for even after the severe frosts of January, our doctor brought us a little bouquet of chrysanthemums, roses, heartsease, and some annuals that had sprung up out of doors and were then in bloom. I have been delighted with its effects in keeping off the inflammatory attacks to which my dear child had been subject previous to our coming here; . . .

I am sorry to be obliged to admit the correctness of your observations with respect to the houses. This invaluable spot has been built upon in the very worst style imaginable, both as to use and ornament. The land has been let in small portions to needy people who have run up cheap small houses for the sake of immediate gain; and consequently there are few houses that afford comfortable accommodation for invalids. It is necessary to seek long and select well. But there are now some better buildings erecting, and the place is likely to be much improved before next winter. The roads of which you complained on behalf of the invalid travellers, are at present under substantial repairs; the shops have become numerous, and the principal hotel, well known to you, is being enlarged, and will have good baths attached to it. There are two other hotels; the Montpelier is by far the most sheltered as to situation. They all supply board as well as lodging, or the latter separately if required. The terms for the two united are two guineas per week for each person, with one guinea for a servant, and for this the fare is very indifferent. The price of lodgings in general is two guineas a week for one sitting room and three bedrooms, including the use of the kitchen, &c. But this price is raised to two guineas and a half in June and to three guineas in July.'

A.B. *Granville,* Spas of England and Principal Sea-bathing Places, (*1841*)

Taming Consumption – Royal National Hospital for Diseases of the Chest

When Ventnor was just beginning to expand in the 1840s Arthur Hill Hassall qualified as a doctor, and it was he who was to found the new chest hospital which opened in 1868. The hospital, which was for all diseases of the chest, was designed to control the spread of the disease by careful management of nursing. It survived for almost one hundred years before the last patients were moved to St. Mary's Hospital, Newport in April 1964.

Hassall's hospital was the first hospital anywhere to be planned providing a separate bedroom for each patient and to be divided up into a number of separate houses or 'cottages'; and its foundation and design evoked much interest in many other places in this country and on the Continent.

The three particular features to which he adhered were firstly that every patient was to have his or her separate room and patients were to associate only in small groups of three or four in sitting rooms when they were ambulant. Secondly, that it was to be a national institution and would accept patients from all over the country and that patients were to be accepted irrespective of their religious beliefs and practices . . . The third condition was that each patient was to make a small contribution to the expenses of the hospital; he reckoned in that way he would be able to accommodate more patients than if it were wholly dependent on charitable donations.

The hospital was built as a series of blocks, each block being made up of two cottages. The blocks were in a straight line and there were in the original plan eight blocks in two groups of four separated by the chapel. Thus each block with its two cottages had six bedrooms on each of the two upper floors and four sitting rooms downstairs. A passage ran east and west the length of the block on each floor giving access to each of the bedrooms or sitting rooms and on the north side of the passage there were bathrooms, wash rooms, ward kitchens or serving kitchens . . .

In the early years milk was evidently regarded as the foundation of an adequate diet as it was later. It was served each morning at eight o'clock, followed by a breakfast of coffee, cocoa, bread and butter, with a cooked dish – bacon, eggs, fried sausage, or fish (bloaters, whiting, haddock, mackerel) once a week and bacon and egg on Saturdays. Dinner always included a meat meal, roast or boiled beef or mutton, meat pie, stewed rabbit and on Sundays cold roast beef; always with vegetables or salad and a pudding to follow, milk pudding, raisin or jam pudding or fruit tart; for tea there was always tea and cocoa, bread and butter; supper was as ordered, details were not given.

E.F. Laidlaw, The Story of the Royal National Hospital Ventnor, (1990)

7 · BESIDE THE SEA

Approaching land is always the most hazardous part of a sea voyage, not least for small boats approaching a new harbour, as these two accounts of harbours in the east and west of the Island reveal.

Bembridge or Brading Haven

Bembridge, or Brading Haven, to give it its older and more attractive name, needs a little careful pilotage because you can't afford to make mistakes in a channel which squeezes in between the rocks surrounding St Helen's Fort on the one side and Bembridge Ledge on the other, or you'll do what a submarine did quite recently and run out of water. The hills above the harbour here are quite lovely but it is only after rounding the last bend that the beauty of the setting really opens out. The haven is a bit like a Roman amphitheatre, dominated by a green hillside which rises steeply on its northern and western sides; [which reminds me – the local Roman villa is really one of the most famous in Britain]. Before the turn of the century we are told :

> 'There were no buoys or beacons . . . other than a few
> withies on the port hand going in, the outer one
> of which rejoiced in the name of "Anthony".'

This one was apparently named after an errant husband whose wife had to chase him across the sands. Cowper speaks of 'the little haven where the church spire admired its own reflection in the still water below'. But in his day it was little more than a marshy swamp with a twisting channel leading to St. Helen's quay. Six years later the authorities reclaimed about 750 acres of land and made quite a decent modern harbour. The entrance is indeed well buoyed, though the bar changes after easterly gales. There is still a white sea mark, the remains of an ancient church, to help us find the entrance buoys and St Helen's quay is there too with a buoyed channel leading up to it. I am, however, making one assumption that is that you can see the buoys among the clutter of boats and distinguish them from unoccupied mooring buoys. I must say, I wouldn't advise picking up a vacant mooring unless you carry legs because the harbour is all very shallow and you will almost certainly dry out; in any case most of the moorings are very light.

If you wish to stay, however, there are two possibilities. One is to find the channel to St Helen's quay where you can dry out comfortably enough on soft mud and incidentally enjoy a friendly welcome from the little Brading Haven Yacht Club. The second, if the wind is off shore and the weather settled, is to anchor just outside, clear of the channel and preferably to the north east of the Fort as suggested by the guide books. I know if you are fairly new to cruising the thought of anchoring in the open is not very attractive because waves can build up and a change of wind can make it extremely uncomfortable. But I shouldn't worry too much because in the Solent area anchoring in the open is taken very much as a matter of course. There is good shelter and as long as you pick your winds you can have a very pleasant night protected by headlands provided you are ready to up anchor to meet a change of wind if necessary.

I mean the great joy of the Solent is that it is relatively sheltered, except in a west or east wind and even then there is always some corner in which you can find adequate protection.

Just before we leave Bembridge, it might be fun to remember that it was on this beach that holystone was first discovered by a bright young first lieutenant in charge of a party collecting sand near the old church. Two or three centuries ago St. Helen's was indeed a popular anchorage for the fleet in days of sail and quite a good centre for provisioning with excellent sweet water and plentiful cheap meat, bread and beer.

David and Joan Hay, The Solent from the Sea, *(1972)*

Entering Newtown Harbour

Though the entrance to Newtown is not difficult, the stranger should approach with care, for shoals run out for some distance from the shore on either hand; that on the port side is specially to be guarded against.

It is useful, also, to bear in mind that the rise of tide here is about nine feet at springs and six feet at neaps. With the lead or sounding-rod employed, the visitor should pick up the leading marks without mishap. These are on our port hand, the eastern side of the channel. The near one is a perch with a Y topmark, standing on the edge of the shoal. The distant one is a black ring having a white centre, standing on the easternmost tip of the land itself. As these two marks come in line, the mariner should have in sight two small buoys, one red, the other black. Leave the red one to port and give the black one a widish berth to starboard, for it marks a gravel spit, which dries out.

One will have sailed between the buoys towards the leading marks for about a quarter of a mile when one will have come up with the entrance, plainly identifiable now from the line of mooring buoys in the main channel, which the chart, but not, I think, elsewhere, goes by the name of Newtown River.

To those acquainted with the place, the devoted Newtownians, all this attempt at direction will seem a needless fussiness. *But I want to see my visitor arrive.* I want to be with him when he takes his first long look at his surroundings.

It will be high-water now, and we are brought up in what looks to be a mighty fine harbour, acre upon acre of clear, clean, still water, land-locked, and sheltered from all the winds that blow. Southwards, inland, the middle distance is marked by a rare clump of pinewood, the land dipping and rising to where Brighstone and Afton Downs form a noble skyline. To the east are frequent knolls of woodland; to the west, across a reedy expanse of oyster beds and old salterns, there is a steeper rise of hills with thicker growth of trees. Scarcely a building is to be seen, nothing at all near at hand, the small church and half-dozen or so dwellings that constitute Newtown being on a slope of land a half-mile from where we lie.

In a few hours' time, though, (come low-water), the scene will be strikingly different. What was at high-water one wide expanse of water is now a system of creeks, seven or eight of them, of which the pleasant

names are Western Haven, Shalfleet Lake, Causeway Lake, Clamerkin
Lake; one must suppose the word lake to be. given from their so different
appearance at flood tide.

There are only two of these creeks in which it is possible for a keel
boat to remain afloat at all states of the tide – namely Clamerkin, and,
where the mooring buoys are, Newtown River itself. Clamerkin can be
considered as separate from the general system; for from Fishouse Point
(on our port hand as we enter the harbour) it wanders away on its own,
for upwards of a mile, in a general easterly and south-easterly direction,
into bird-haunted solitudes.

John Scott Hughes, Harbours of the Solent, *(1956)*

The Needles

It had been in my mind to mention a couple of unusual views I had
recently of the Needles, when I reflected that during a lifetime of
seafaring – threaded I could even say, through those Needles – I have
never known them to have an appearance other than unusual and
extraordinary, so endless are the effects of sunshine and cloud on these
great chalk masses, moulded by time to such nobleness of form.

Traditionally the name 'Needles' derives from a fourth outlying rock,
a thin spire of chalk 120 feet high, which fell in 1764. All the books have
this date pat, which suggests that something remarkable attended the
event; and indeed many agree that it was struck by lightning. The three
main rocks which have since constituted the group have been likened in
shape to 'great chalk haystacks'. A more striking comparison and apter,
I think, sees in them a resemblance to the lower jawbone of some vast
sea-monster, the teeth awash; and this much less fanciful from a lower
and nearer viewpoint, when you plainly see that not one of the three rises
squarely from its base, but that each slopes evenly upwards to a sharp
ridge, or rather, continuing the comparison, to a cutting-edge.

What gives the Needles their grandeur, and often, towards evening, a
sublimity, is that they are framed or cupped in by that cliff (strikingly
named Main Bench) at which the Island's downland terminates with
such abrupt magnificence, 'the grandest chalk precipice in southern
England'.

John Scott Hughes, Harbours of the Solent, *(1956)*

The Needles Lighthouse

The first Needles lighthouse to protect the dangerous coast showed its light in 1786, but still ships were lost. Its site on the Needles Headland was 462 feet above sea level and it was often shrouded in fog at the very time when guidance was needed, but it continued in service until 1859 when the present lighthouse was built.

The present Needles lighthouse was and still is a dramatic triumph of human engineering over one of the most hostile natural environments on the British coast. It was James Walker who had the vision to imagine dynamiting a platform into the furthest of the Needle stacks.

The Needles lighthouse, a 109 foot (33.25m) circular granite tower, was built to withstand hurricane force winds and waves up to 20ft high. The lighthouse base was stepped to break the waves and the massive walls built a yard thick at the base tapering to 1½ feet (61cm) thick at the top of the tower.

As the three-man crew could be cut off from the Island for weeks at a time by some of our choicest spells of weather, to supply them a 2,400 gallon water-tank and a coal store had to be blasted out of the interior of the stack.

The 35,000 candle-power light of the Needles has a range of 17 miles, reflecting as red white or green depending on the position of the observer, the green light showing the safe channel. It is easily identified by its own pattern of two second flashes followed by fourteen seconds of darkness. Local residents are more familiar with the foghorn which keeps us company with mournful double blasts every 22 seconds in cloudy and foggy weather.

It sometimes took a fortnight for the crew to reach the coal store. In really rough weather, despite the stepped base, the waves crashed high up the tower. One keeper was on the phone, over 40 feet up, when a wave came through the window and washed his breakfast off the table. Sometimes the spray of a wave can reach the lantern . . .

One wonders at how the men got on, living in close quarters in their small circular world. Tony Isaacs, who used to bring the daily papers and 'sticky doughnuts on Saturdays', told me that he only knew of one keeper taken off. 'I think it was falling out over a cricket match.'

During the 1990s Trinity House adopted a policy of automating all the lighthouses around Britain and modernising them with new equipment. The old glass lantern was replaced with a helicopter pad which allows the tower to be manned in emergencies.

In September 1993 an electric cable was laid from the Old Battery down the cliff, along a trench, threaded through the solid rock of the last Needle to replace the 100 DC generator with a 415 v mains (thereby contradicting the old saying about the Seven Wonders of the Island which includes 'The Needles you cannot thread'). The whole exercise cost an estimated £352,000.

Following a special ceremony on December 6th, 1994, the last two crew finally left their granite abode on December 8th, thus bringing to an end 135 years of self-contained human isolation on the Needles rocks. It also marked the end of 208 years of manned lighthouse keeping on the Needles Peninsula.

John. C. Medland, MSc, Alum Bay and the Needles, *(1995)*

Mackerel

'As mackerel fishing now seems a thing of the past, and the mackerel fishers are gone . . . I will try and describe the activities of the time, which was eagerly looked forward to by all concerned as a means of settling up the winter's bills. The fish were usually punctual in their arrival in the bay between the 7th and 15th of May, and, as they came as a thief in the night, a good look out was kept. The old hands would be seen along the cliff-top looking for signs that denoted their arrival, such as beds of bait, seagulls busy, large oily patches on the water, and, above all, the shoals of fish themselves. Sometimes they would be seen miles out, at others close in, but wherever it was it meant the men must be alert, for, as they used to say, 'Fish and tide wait for no man.' As soon as the shoals were seen to be looking well, word would be sent round to the extra hands needed, who would at once make their way to the shore to get the nets and boats ready. There were three places in Chale Bay where the gangs worked from – Blackgang two boats, Ladder two boats, Atherfield several boats, while often a large gang would come round from Sandown to Atherfied to help. Boats and nets being ready, a keen look-out was kept, as the first catch meant the best market. There were at each place one or two look-outs, who kept high up on the cliffs, and at the sight of shoals of fish close in, would call the boats afloat and into the shots, which were the places free of rocks where nets could be used. 'Look-out' would be shouted by the watcher, and away would go the crew, straining every nerve and putting out every ounce of strength, in an endeavour to head the fish. Most of them were four-oared boats, with one hand to shoot the net over the stern, and it was a sight to be remembered to see the four hefty fellows straighten out at the oars, putting every once of strength into it, fairly lifting the boat out of the water, and the net trailing over the stern.

I well remember such a scene late in the evening of May 10th 1902, at Blackgang, with the late Maurice Wheeler's crew. The large shoal of fish had been playing in and out for a long time, but kept just out of shot. Presently the head of the shoal came a bit nearer. 'Now or never!' shouted Maurice, 'Go on,' and they started and in a very few minutes the boat was flying out as the fish were coming towards the shore, but when they started to go out again the net was in the way and they were soon landed, some thousands in number. Even when the fish were hemmed in by the net it did not mean they were caught, as at times the bottom line of the net would beach and tear, or a small rock would go through it, and the fish would soon see the smallest hole and be at liberty. Then again, with a strong tide running and too many energetic helpers, the bottom of the net would lift and the fish would escape.

As soon as it was seen that the fish were enclosed it was very necessary to keep the weight of them in the middle of the net, where the meshes were finer and stronger, and as this part of the net reached shore four or five of the hands would go down behind it to ease the strain – and what a wetting they got, as, of course did the helpers; in fact, that added to the fun, and even the lady helpers were proud to be able to say they were wet through.

The most exciting moments perhaps are when the fish, hemmed round by the net, are being landed on the beach. The huge mass jumps furiously about, their gorgeous colours flashing, and every helper getting covered with scales from them. The fish are packed up in boxes or baskets and rapidly taken to market. While a few of the crew go off with the fish, the others get the net sorted out and back in the boat ready for the next lot, as, fish like tides, wait for no man, and are here today and gone tomorrow. – they will not wait to be caught.

Fred Mew, Back of the Wight, (*1951*)

Lifeboats Come to Bembridge and Brighstone

It was not until 1867 that the Institution (R.N.L.I) decided to place a lifeboat at Bembridge, and I believe that decision was implemented by the courageous rescue of the Norwegian barque *Egbert* by the fishermen of Bembridge in an ordinary open boat. This ship, loaded with barley, had run aground on Bembridge Ledge during a hard easterly gale, and the crew were in imminent peril from heavy seas, which were breaking over her, and, as usual, had taken to the rigging. A house-to-house call went round the village, and a party of volunteers set off for the wreck in an open boat belonging to the War Office. Their efforts were completely successful, and the whole crew was brought safely ashore, including one small boy who was too scared to come down from aloft, and who had to be carried down to the boat by one of the Bembridge men. This spectacular rescue so excited the citizens of Worcester that they subscribed a sufficient sum of money to pay for a lifeboat and presented it to the Institution to be placed at Bembridge, and very rightly named the said boat 'City of Worcester'.

Captain R.C. Watson, Hon. Sec. R.N.L.I., Annals of Bembridge Lifeboats and Bembridge Lifeboatmen – *held at Lord Louis Library, Newport.*

'It is a matter of painful notoriety, that 14 lives were lost by shipwreck at the back of the Island, about three weeks ago. It was stated by the officers of coastguard and others at the Inquest, that if a life-boat had been at hand, the whole of these lives might have been saved.'

These opening lines from an appeal letter date 24th December 1859 signed by Edward MacAll the Rural Dean and Rector of Brighstone and George Pellow Gaze, the Rector of Brook, sets the scene for the beginning of the life-boat service in Brighstone Bay . . . So the two Rectors launched their appeal . . . The response was so encouraging that six weeks later on 4th February 1860 they were able to write again [to the R.N.L.I.] saying the money was forthcoming . . .

A further development was that the Royal Victoria Yacht Club, without previous concert, embarked on a similar scheme to provide a life-boat on the South Wight coast . . . the Commodore of the R.V.Y.C., Mr Holland-Ackers [sent] an appeal circular to all the members and the money was forthcoming. Congratulations all round were in order and so the life-boat service came to Brook and Brighstone . . .

When the call came a gun was fired and the crew would hurry to the life-boat stations together with a beach handling party of villagers. In the case of Brook and Brighstone Grange the carters working in the fields would bring down their horses. The boat would be hauled stern first to the beach by a team of up to eight horses, depending on the weather, and the crew would embark. The boat on its carriage was then taken as far as possible into the sea before being turned by the leading horses, so that the bow was pointing directly at the oncoming waves breaking on the shore.

A successful launch depended on three important factors. First, and most important, the coxswain had to choose exactly the right moment to give the order 'Launch'. The incoming wave had to be big enough to float the boat, but not so large as to overwhelm it, also the area of water had to be large enough to enable the boat to go ahead into deep water.

Secondly, the helpers, often standing in the sea, had to react instantly and together when the coxswain's cry came to launch, by hauling on the lines which shot the boat forward off the carriage into the sea using all their weight and strength. For a good launch 60 or more people were needed.

Thirdly, the ability of ten oarsmen to be ready to pull together with their oars was crucial. It was also essential that they made their second stroke before the oncoming wave hit the boat.

Christopher J. Willis and Edward H. Roberts, The Lifeboats of Brighstone Bay, *(1986)*

The eastern and western ends of the Island are, in many ways, mirror images. Both are almost islands, both have great cliffs of chalk, both have exposed Wealden sands – at Brook in west Wight and, more dramatically, at Redcliff in Sandown Bay. They create a dramatic meeting of sea and land and on the shore are the bays, small and often dangerous on the western coast, gloriously expansive at Sandown.

Freshwater Cliffs

This account of the scene at Freshwater in the last year of the eighteenth century could only have been written by a middle-class visitor. He found it impossible to believe that a man would risk his life in collecting eggs and birds from the cliff face for the small amount of money he gained.

But with bread prices at famine levels and a wage of only 8s (40p) a week to keep a family a labourer might well face the dangers for the extra pence.

The sheep that were on the down made the scene picturesque; they approached the verge of the cliff without fear, and browsed the scanty blade which grew on it. The height of these cliffs exceeds those of Culver, at the extremity of Brading Down, having 600 feet; and, viewed from the sea, astonish the spectator by their immensity. During a certain period of the year a great variety of marine birds, among which, I was told, puffins, eider ducks, razorbills, willocks (guillemot) gulls, cormorants, Cornish choughs, daws, starlings and wild pigeons, frequent the cliff, to deposit their eggs among the inaccessible places of the rock, and breed free of all intrusion.

But of late the adventurous peasant descends by a rope, fixed to an iron bar, to plunder the birds of their eggs, and take such as come within his reach. This is a perilous expedient, and the advantage unequal to the danger; a dozen birds yield only one pound of soft feathers, which is sold to the merchant for 8d (3p), and the carcasses are bought by the fishermen, at 6d (2p) a dozen to bait their crabpots. Thus a daring adventurer suffers himself to hover over destruction, for several hours, to gain a precarious advantage. In the same way samphire is gathered from the middle of these precipices. No doubt there must be some greater inducement than gain; so trifling a sum will never tempt a man to hazard his life, 'tis the fame they acquire by undertaking these hardy exploits that impels them forward, and the pleasure of recounting over their deeds to a listening circle sufficiently repays them for the danger.
The Hampshire Repository, vol II 1799 - 1801

Hazel Nuts at Brook

William Schellinks, was a Dutch painter and engraver working in the last quarter of the seventeenth century. On 13 September 1662 he crossed from Southampton to Cowes and three days later he was riding from Shorwell to Brook where he saw the hazel nut beds in the cliff, but in a far more extensive state than they are today. Schellinks attributed the fate of these trees to 'the deluge' – The biblical Flood – and their local name continues to remember this seventeenth century observation.

On the 16th September we rode in the morning from Shorwell back to Brighstone and from there to the village of Brook, and down to a plain called Brook Green, from where a broad ditch, 2 or 3 miles long, runs towards the sea, which, in summer is without water and almost dry. In the ground, or rather on both sides of this ditch, 25 or 30 feet, and nearer the sea 50 to 60 feet down below ground level, one sees and finds some very large hazelnut trees with their branches, leaves and nuts, which are fully grown. There is no other explanation, how they could have got so deeply into the ground, but that they were covered with earth by the deluge, which prevented the air from reaching them, and in this way they were preserved for ever. We took two men and a boy with us with a shovel and two pickaxes, but did not have much trouble with digging, as we found them in the ground, trees, branches and nuts, in the loose broken ground. We found many so fresh and hard, as if they had not long been lying there, but most of the nuts broke up if one did not handle them gently like rotten wood. We took some of them with us as a keepsake. At a gentleman's house very close to this place they show the antler of a deer, which was also found in this ground.

The Journal of William Schellinks' Travels in England 1661-1663, (1993)

Another interesting feature can be seen in the cliff at Brook. About six feet down from the top of the cliff there is a band of gravel in which there is a dark band of peaty material. On inspection this proves to consist of large numbers of hazel-nuts, acorn and alder cones, together with leaves, twigs and branches of various sizes. These must have been deposited on the banks of upper reaches of the Western Yar, some 7000 years ago, when there was still a considerable area of land to the south, which has since been eroded by the sea. Local people aptly refer to them as 'Noah's Nuts'. They are not fossilised but perfectly preserved even to the extent of having discernible tooth-marks made by rodents.

Oliver Frazer, The Natural History of the Isle of Wight, (1990)

Luccombe Chine

The walk at low water from Shanklin to Luccombe Chine is very pleasant. Luccombe Chine is one of those places (common to every route taken by tourists) which are unaccountably neglected, though equally beautiful with other much praised spots. Here is Luccombe Chine, only second to that of Shanklin, and not one tourist in a hundred of those who visit Shanklin sets an eye upon Luccombe. Indeed, it is most picturesque, and for those who love the natural without any intrusion of the artificial, Luccombe Chine is the most delightful in the Isle. Viewed from the shore, it is singularly sweeping and beautiful, piled up superbly. But its entrance from above is quite unassuming. It suddenly sinks out of a field in the most unpretentious manner, opening out far below the upper level. No sign post tells of its existence and the preference of humanity is feebly represented by a few cottages.

The author of this extract, J. Redding Ware, had seen the relatively new Military Road along the coast to Freshwater and he was conscious of the problems the engineers had overcome, but he was also aware of the long term triumph of nature. This we can see today where a new piece of road has been constructed between Brook and Freshwater, some yards back from the old road. But already the prospect of this disappearing and with it the use of the Military Road to traffic looms ahead.

Along the south coast of the island, and the line of the chines, great attention was given by the military engineers who controlled the making of the road from Freshwater to Blackgang, now about twenty years since, to arrest the rapid action of even a very narrow stream of water under favourable circumstances in cutting a chine. The road is in some parts carried over chines at a height of over two hundred feet. It was therefore necessary to stop the action of the water upon the land, or the wasting away of the foundations of the viaducts was but a question of time – a question which nature holds in little respect. The chine-cutting brooks, over which the road passes, were consequently confined to artificial channels, and the danger is at all events postponed.
J. Redding Ware, The Isle of Wight, (*1875*)

Alum Bay and Coloured Sands

Many will remember a visit to Alum Bay, the descent to the shore, and the pleasure of collecting your own coloured sand to fill a bottle and take home a souvenir of this remarkable cliff face. All this has long since gone as the danger of the crumbling surface made regulation inevitable. Hubert Poole saw the Bay when it was untouched by modern development but when it was already a tourist attraction.

The coloured sands of Alum Bay have long been regarded as one of the wonders of the Island and its white glasshouse sands, though no longer used, were once upon a time a notable export to London, Bristol, Runcorn and Sunderland. These strata of varied colours and shades appear in the high cliffs of Alum Bay in a vertical position having been stood on end during that time when the more obvious wrinkles, such as the Alps and Himalayas, appeared on the face of the earth. In addition to their vertical position the strata have varying degrees of hardness and their exposed faces have answered in an uneven manner to the onslaughts of wind and rain. They accordingly stand away from and overlap each other much in the manner of the flats used on either side of the stage in theatrical scenery.

To view the effect at its best, a position at the top of the Chalk cliff at the southern end of the bay should be chosen, though not one in a thousand visitors has ever seen it from this point of view, owing to the stiff climb and the limited time allowed by the coaches. If the bay can be viewed after a shower, or whilst the cliffs are still wet from recent rain the effect is more brilliant. Wind, by drying the cliff face and distributing loose sand over the veins of the brighter colours tends to dull the general effect. In the bay itself sufficient distance from the cliff cannot be obtained to see more than a portion at a time, in other words, you cannot see the cliffs for the sand. However, the sand and not the scenery appears to be the great attraction.

Through the long summer days motor-coach after motor coach deposits its load of warm humanity at the top of the cliff. Shorewards the passengers hurry and commence an attack with claws and knives on the cliff face, the offensive being carried out for the purpose of filling bottles with layers of sand of various colours.

In any future statistics regarding coastal erosion of the Island the amount of coloured sand removed from Alum Bay by its summer visitors will have to be taken into account.

Hubert H. Poole, Come and see my Island *(1935). Typescript held by the Lord Louis Library, Newport.*

Totland Bay

Totland was created for the Edwardian holiday visitor. Built on an open heath, just round the corner from Yarmouth, it attracted middle class families of comfortable means who took a house for the summer, brought the servants and enjoyed a sybaritic, open-air life.

Totland Bay . . . I remember what that had been like in the 'nineties, with the sea-front alive with gaily clad people; the men in straw hats and wonderful blazers gallanting partners also in straw hats, with leg-of-mutton sleeves that produced the effect of a perpetual shrug. And there were the long rows of bathing machines, from which these same partners would emerge in costumes of such multifold decency that it is wonderful how any of them contrived to swim a stroke - if any of them ever did, for I do not seem to remember them ever doing much more than jumping and splashing about in shallow water. Even so, it was considered almost dangerously advanced for them to be thus employed, and habited, in the company of men.

But then Totland was nothing if not up-to-date. Its dominating and symbolic feature was one of the new luxury hotels that were the very latest thing in Victorian architecture; all turrets and gables and balconies and red brick and white paint . . .

The atmosphere of Totland in the summer seemed to be that of a non-stop regatta, of which the formal event was only the culminating episode.
Esmé Wingfield-Stratford, Before the lamps went out, *(1945)*

A Long Summer Day at Seaview

On a fine morning (and all August mornings were fine in Seaview when I was young!) each family's advance guard would appear soon after nine o'clock to open the tent, set out deck chairs and spread towels within the small territory defined by the tent's frontage. The main party, bearing supplies probably completed by calls at Watson's and Henley's, the High Street bakers, would arrive an hour or two later. As the tide dictated the day's activities and pauses recurred – 'Not enough water at the raft and diving board? – Why not see if Mr. Churchill has a boat free?' – 'Any one for cricket?' – 'Let's put up the quoits net before someone pinches that pitch!' – 'Look, the Queen Mary! Isn't she lovely?' – 'That's the Pilot boat coming back.' And so on till the trees in the gardens behind the wall begin to shade the top of the beach and it's time to fetch a tray of tea from the cafe by Gully Road and, in later August at least, start wasp swatting. 'No dear, bring your bathing things back to dry for tomorrow.' – 'Did you remember to tie up the tent door?'

My wife's family usually took a walk after supper; the age of owner-drivers was only just beginning and few families brought cars to Seaview. Along the beach again and up over the Priory fields to St. Helen's Church; across the fields from Nettlestone to Bullen; along the Duver to Puckpool or up Oakhill Road to Pondwell – there were many routes to choose from, all offering somewhere the prospect of fields and woods and sea under the sun's parting benediction. Often there would be something on at the Pavilion in the evening – a concert party, a cinema show, dancing, and later in the evening everyone seemed to take a stroll down the High Street and along the Esplanade. We sat on the wall watching the passers-by and the goings-on in what became the Starboard Club but was then a private house usually occupied in August by a lively young family. The Seaview Hotel Bar and Belvoir cafe were busy until closing time.

G. *Parsloe*, A Present from Seaview, (*1979*)

Seagrove Bay, Seaview in the 1930s

The pier was used regularly by the steamers bringing day-trippers from Clarence and Southsea piers. The beach in those days seemed to be very sandy - the steps leading down to it at Woodside numbered about 14, not the three or four there are there now, and the shingle was almost non-existent . . . My father, Mr. Wilson Bull, owned the tents and deckchairs – the tents lined the sea wall and when the spring tides came Father regularly patrolled the beach during the night to make sure they were not washed away. The tents were erected in about April, and taken down during September or October. The season seemed to be longer in those days. Mr. Frank Punch and my uncle Mr. George White helped with collecting money and stacking the deckchairs at the end of the day. Father spent a good deal of his time making and repairing the deckchairs, using an old treadle sewing machine . . .

Seaview was a renowned holiday resort, with a large number of bed and breakfast and full board facilities. My mother ran one of the latter; her season began in April and ended in October. It was very hard work. Some of her guests brought their own food for Mother to prepare and cook, paying only for the use of the rooms. Others had inclusive terms – this she preferred. In those days a full breakfast, packed lunch, tea and three course dinner were provided. My mother, father, brother and myself slept in one bedroom, the guests having the other three, plus bathroom, dining room and sitting room. We had only the kitchen and scullery.

Isle of Wight Federation of Women's Institutes, Isle of Wight within Living Memory, (*1994*)

Brighstone Holiday Camp

The holiday camp thrived in the period following the Second World War, but its foundation lies in the pre-war period as the camp at Brighstone shows. Here the campers enjoyed a very healthy holiday which involved a fair amount of walking as they went back and forth from the village.

Built in 1929-31 by Mr Edwards and Mrs Sleep. The first camp to be built on the Island, and the first of its kind. There were 140 chalets which could hold about 400 people. The camp was built in one of three fields, one for camping and the other for a sports field which had a football pitch going out towards the sea. This has now completely gone.

Now to get there in those days was London to Ryde by train, and bus to Brighstone village, or to the camp. Those who arrived in the village could have their luggage picked up by an old lorry and then they took a stroll along the country lane to the camp. Many would come by bike or tandem from London . . . Throughout the week they would be taken for a stroll around the village, always stopping in the village for a cup of tea in the tearoom before returning to the camp.

The camp was taken over by the army to house about a 1000 troops to man the new gun site on the cliff [and in] 1945 the camp was handed back to Camper Ltd. With a new boss, young Mr Sleep took over and it reopened in 1946. Now it was only chalets, no tents, and became a family camp. Over the years families came back year after year, each time bringing more people. One couple came back for 45 years and they knew so many local people because they loved walking round the village. The young men of the village would play the campers at cricket on a Sunday afternoon and even take part in the concert on Thursday night. Many local people were employed as staff. As a family camp there was no Bar so if you wanted a drink, it was a walk to the village, and a talk with the locals, which many people did . . .

On a Sunday morning there was a walk to the village and it was quite a picture to see some 300 people all head up the lane under Mike Guy. On Wednesday there was a longer walk which wove its way through the lanes to the Longstone and to the top of Mottistone Down and downhill to Brighstone chalk pit. There awaiting them would be tea and cakes – a well earned break before a walk back to the camp for the evening meal.

Brighstone Village Museum Trust, Brighstone Village Isle of Wight, (2004)

Coloured Sand Souvenirs

At the end of the eighteenth century some unknown artist began to create pictures using Alum Bay coloured sands and these became a fashion among wealthy art patrons. In the first half of the nineteenth century a wider public was able to buy small sand pictures and take them home as reminders of their visit to the island.

The smaller, and cruder, pictures, the average size being that of a picture postcard, . . . can be looked upon as having filled the niche now occupied by the lettered peppermint rock and picture postcard, that is they made inexpensive souvenirs of a visit to the Island . . .

These smaller sand-pictures, which are truly an Island craft, aimed at reproducing its topography and but rarely ventured into any more fanciful subject . . . Several different workers were producing these pictures, the best known being J. Neat, who rose to the dignity of a label informing the public that this 'Isle of Wight Curiosity is Executed in Natural colour sand taken from Alum Bay by J. Neat, St Thomas's Square, Newport, I.W.'

Only a small proportion of the pictures are signed but in examining a quantity the unsigned examples will be found to fall into a small number of separate styles of execution, most probably denoting a similar number of artists. A few are dated, 'Osborne House before rebuilding', by E. Dore, 'Newport' is dated 1844, and one of the 'Castle Keep', artist unknown, was produced in 1854. 'The Needles' by Ed. Dore 1840 is the earliest, and 'Blackgang Chine' 1855 by an unknown artist is the latest of this series I have seen. It would appear that they were being freely made and sold about the middle of the nineteenth century.

Another form in which sand was displayed was in glass bottles of an elongated bell shape. These were made in several sizes, the smaller holding sand unevenly layered in contrasting colours, whilst the larger had the addition of a small crude view, usually the Needles, painted in sand on the inside of the bottle, with layered sand as a background . . .

The older bottles were largely made, or filled, by J. Neat, who might well call attention to his pictures being formed of sand in its natural colour, for some colours are absent from the cliffs, such as green in its brighter shades. Where nature has failed art has entered and many of the pictures by the older exponents of the craft, owe their brighter shades to paint applied to the sand.

The present-day exponent of the craft is Mr. R.J. Snow, of Lake, though, as the finished picture is retailed at a very low price there is not much scope for him to show his undoubted artistic ability. He describes his results as 'Souvenir Pictures'. I can only say that at the price they are wonderfully good, and one may be sure of having the genuine thing for he uses the sands and clays finely sifted in their natural colours only, without the aid of artificial colouring whatever. Each picture is made by painting in gum, the sand being applied to this whilst still wet by means of an ordinary mustard spoon.

Hubert H. Poole, Come and see my Island, *(1935). Typescript held at Lord Louis Library, Newport.*

8 · GETTING ABOUT

Until very recent times most working people, and in the Island that would mean country people, could rely only on their feet to get them from place to place and many would not move more than a few miles. Farmers would harness up their horses to take the cart or trap to Newport for the markets on Wednesday and Saturday and from these necessary trips evolved one of the country services that transformed life in distant communities – the carrier.

The Country Carrier on the Isle of Wight generally traded from his home location to Newport and back, with some going between the towns on the eastern coast of the Island. The areas they covered represented a kind of 'wedge' with the points of each section meeting at Newport where all the Carriers met and exchanged goods for other areas. Loyalty forbad one Carrier journeying into another's territory, and charges for their services were similar for all Carriers on the Isle of Wight .

The Carrier was basically a person who served the country areas, providing transport for both goods, animals and people to and from home and the nearest town. Most of the early Carriers on the Isle of Wight were small farmers, or small holders, who needed to transport their own produce to other people locally, and into the towns, for sale. The small holder farmer who was already making a regular trip into Newport for market day, on Saturday, often had room on his cart for additional items, and friends. They needed to buy the families (sic.)

requirements from the town, so he started to carry goods for others who either could not afford the money or more probably the time, to travel, but who had goods to sell, and who needed goods purchased – and charging a fee or 'carriage' for his trouble. The length of time on the journey, the often inclement weather, and the need to keep 'other peoples' goods and indeed the passengers reasonably dry and warm, led to a canvas tilt being fixed over the farm wagon with canvas sheets which could either be pulled across or rolled up, both at the back and front, and a chain supported tail board at the rear.

So was established a form of transport which in many ways survived long after horse drawn vehicles had departed and been replaced by motor vehicles in the 20th century, and right until the last Carrier stopped trading in the 1960s . . .

From the early years of Carriers, there were only three ways of contacting them; by word of mouth, by post, or with 'The Flag'. It was the flag which was the most common method of attracting the Carriers attention. To indicate that the householder required his services, a flag made from any piece of cloth or rag, or a duster, would be attached to a stick which would be placed in the hedge, or tied to the garden gate by the roadside, or even at the end of the lane leading to the customers house.

To ensure the correct Carrier called at the customers house, and to save an unnecessary stop, a specifically coloured flag was used by each Carrier. The procedure the Carrier adopted on seeing his flag was to call at the house, taking the flag out of the hedge or the gate . . . it must never be left, as it was a signal to others that the Carrier had not called . . . and when one wanted to travel as a passenger with the Carrier, that he was expected.

Whilst the collection and delivery of goods was the major part of the Carriers trade, the provision of a shopping service was vital to many who lived in the country. Clothes, medicine and specialised items could only be purchased in the towns and were often needed urgently . . . Clothes are very personal things but the Carrier would be asked to buy items for all the family, on appro (on approval) and the selection was sometimes left to the Carrier to fit the family out with suitable clothes.

Food was another area where the Carrier might well be left to select items for his customers on a regular basis. Several customers on Arthur Sprake's route left the selection of their Sunday joint entirely to him, and similarly with a fish meal which for many was on Friday. A close relationship built up between the butcher, pork butcher or fish monger, and the Carrier, who often found a choice cut put aside specifically for him . . .

The charge or 'carriage' for providing any Carrier service was quite small, certainly between the Wars. 3d (1½p) or 6d (2½p) was quite normal for delivering a mall parcel anywhere, and after the War, 6d or 1/- (5p). There was no set tariff, the price often being agreed according to the persons ability to pay. The barter system was quite common. Payment to the Carrier might well be in the form of vegetables, eggs or other items.

St. Thomas's Square, [Newport] was known as the Carrier's Square. The location was central to the town, and in close proximity to a number of Hotels and Inns which provided Carriers with a base for messages and for passengers awaiting their arrival. These Inns provided   livery facilities (stabling, feeding and watering of horses and a resting place for them) . . .

The use of the Square by the Carriers continued through the transition from horses to motor vehicles but had ended by the time of the Second World War they were becoming a nuisance to some of the local shopkeepers and tradesmen, who by now were starting to use their own transport to carry their goods.

Derek Sprake, Put Out the Flag, The Story of the Isle of Wight Carriers 1860-1960 *(1993)*.

A Special Parcel

In 1920 an eight year old girl, Freda Streets became part of the Sprakes' parcels.

In the summer of 1920 [John Bull] invited Freda to come to Chale and stay with him and his wife for a holiday. Freda's mother took her to Newport [from East Cowes] with her belongings in a straw case and left her in St. Thomas's Square to await the Carrier. She had a label tied to her coat giving her name and destination, and she was sat at Sprake's post in the Square on her little box, and waited for Percy Sprake to arrive. Mr. Bull had told him that he would have a 'special' item to deliver that day, and on arrival Freda was lifted up onto the seat, and a rug was put round her knees to keep her warm.

On the eight mile journey to Chale they called at lots of houses and farms delivering all sorts of goods, and the journey took a long time. On the way they stopped at the home of a Mrs. Buckett where Freda was given a cup of cold tea, and taken to the toilet. On arrival at her destination, Mr. and Mrs. Bull were waiting for her and on being lifted down from the van, she was handed over with the friendly comment – 'Here's your little maid, John'. All part of the Carrier's job.

Derek Sprake, Put Out the Flag, The Story of the Isle of Wight Carriers 1860-1960 (*1993*).

The Railway Men

In 1923 the separate railway companies in the Island were absorbed by Southern Railways, but there remained very much an Island ethos among the men employed by the company. A family atmosphere is what comes through and in their personal reminiscences we can share that sense of companionship in their work. The next three items are all taken from volume 2 of Andrew Britton's Once Upon a Line.

Birds, Beasts and Flowers on the Line

Richard (Dick) Russell

Many stories of life in the signalboxes on the Island concerned animals and birds. Firstly, there was the station cat at Sandown. Very artful this one, calling at the signalbox for milk, then the porter's room, and then the booking office. He would jump under trains entering and leaving the station and come up the other side having narrow escapes most days. He would get among the trucks during shunting operations and although most of the staff were wise to it he frightened some of the passengers waiting for their trains on the platform. After all that he died of cat flu! The chap who had the job of burying him on a piece of waste ground put up a cross and epitaph as follows: Here lies the body of poor 'Tiger Tim' – the trains all missed him but the flu got him.

At that time Syd Dennett, the signalman at Merstone on my turn, had a pigeon named Bill. This bird would go to work with him, either perched on his shoulder as he cycled down the road or fluttering along just behind him. It was Syd's practice on the early turn to shut Bill up in the brake van of the early goods train, with instructions to the guard to let him out at Sandown to fly back to Merstone. This went off all right for a time, until one morning Syd rang up asking where Bill was. 'On the station roof,' I replied. 'Well chase him off,' said Syd. This I did but Bill flew round for a few minutes and then took up the same position. Then, when the Newport train ran in he jumped on the roof of one of the coaches and had a ride back to Merstone. He never did fly back again but waited for the next train. One morning he even rode back on the roof of the driver's cab of the engine. I expected him to take off when the train got round the corner, but he stuck it out all the way to Merstone. Syd got fed up with sending him after that.

We sometimes had a consignment of calves from the mainland who came on one of the early trains from Ryde, and they had to be transferred to the train for Merstone. They were nice little creatures and as they had rope halters on we used to lead them round like dogs one at a time. Then one of the Merstone guards decided he could take two. He got them nearly to his train when something frightened them and they bolted, one going one side of a post and the other around the other side, doing considerable damage to the guard's nose. He never tried that again.

There was a flower traffic from Newchurch to Covent Garden. The flowers were packed in cardboard boxes, but there were no special vans for these. They were loaded in the trains vans, sometimes up to the roof, hardly leaving room for the guard to get in, and all these had to be transferred to the Ryde train at Sandown. Officially there was only one porter to do this, but I have sometimes known nine chaps working away at it. I have known the porter (whose job it was), the signalman(me), the driver, the fireman and the guard of the Ryde train, the driver, fireman, and guard of the Newport train together with the chap out of the parcels office, all mucking in to keep delays to a minimum, and to get the flowers to Covent Garden on time.

Ventnor town station seems to have been 'Summoned by Bells'.

Percy Primer
I started work at Ventnor Town Station in 1929, and can well remember the 'Five Minute Bell' in use. You will of course be aware of the steep approach to Ventnor Station, and the practice of ringing a large hand bell outside the station, five minutes before the departure of the train,

was done for the benefit of those intending passengers still coming up the hill. As far as I know, the bell remained at the station until closure. The menacing sound of the bell would give heavily laden tourists, weighed down with luggage a minor heart attack as they panicked to struggle up to the station!

Perhaps not so well known was the unusual conveyance used to carry invalid passengers from the train to the taxis at Ventnor Town. The Royal National Hospital for Diseases of the Chest was located at Ventnor. As a result we had plenty of invalids to cope with at times. However, instead of a wheelchair as is in use at most terminal stations today, we had a chair with four short legs and four handles, two at the front and two at the back, rather like a sedan chair. I well remember conveying the late Ralph Vaughan Williams, the composer, in this way.

One item of unusual equipment is that of the portable footbridge at Ventnor Town Station until the closure in April 1966. It was positioned when in use between platforms one and two. The bridge was a cumbersome affair and required two men to put it into place. There was an interesting procedure in using the footbridge, which was only introduced in about 1936; there was a bell code in conjunction with the signal box situated at the entrance to the tunnel, because the bridge would be across the main running line. If there was a train waiting to depart in the number two platform, which could not leave until after the incoming train had arrived on number one platform, then obviously the bridge had to be removed at a given time. So before the signalman would accept a train from Wroxall, he would ring a bell on the platform and the bridge would be removed. We would then ring a repeating bell indicating that the bridge had been removed. All was then clear for the arriving train.

Royal Train Passengers

Readers should notice particularly the 'Island railway custom'.

Alexander Wheway
After Queen Victoria died the Royals rarely frequented Osbourne (sic.) House. However, they did visit the Isle of Wight for Cowes Week and on special occasions like the naval reviews. One particular story comes to mind concerning the two small princesses, some time before World War II. The driver of the Cowes to Newport train spotted two small figures

with a tall lady on the platform of Cowes station, as he puffed away out of the platform towards Newport. Now the lady hailed the departing train to stop, and naturally, as was the Island railway custom, he halted his train and reversed back. He collected his grateful passengers and continued on his short journey to Newport, thinking little more of this everyday occurrence. Upon arrival at Newport the stationmaster greeted the three passengers 'bowing and scraping' all the way. Now the driver, whose name was 'Bonnie' Baines, and guard Harry Groves, later discovered from me at Sandown who their passengers were. I had received a telephone message from Newport informing me that the passengers were no less than Princess Elizabeth (later to become Queen Elizabeth) and Princess Margaret.

Andrew Britton, Once Upon a Line vol 2, (1984)

Bringing a Car to the Island

The motor car would have been a rare sight in the Island in the early twentieth century but visitors did come with their cars on a regular time-table. It was only when the driver decided to take an unusual crossing that he might run into trouble, as one discovered in 1903.

Captain Bowman writing in *The Car*, says: Undoubtedly the easiest journey to the Isle of Wight is from Southampton to Cowes (cost 22s 6d – £1.10). No tidal difficulties arise, the car can be driven on board the steamer, and no delays occur either on embarking or on arrival at Cowes. Both the other routes involve shipping the car on a barge, a rather delicate operation according to the state of the tide. Unfortunately, too, one must cross before noon or early in the afternoon. The belated motorist who had a puncture or other minor misfortunate if he arrives after 1.30p.m., will greatly resent having to leave his car overnight in Portsmouth. If he be tempted to seek out a special route for himself this narrative may dissuade him.

Some time ago, having occasion to cross with my car to the Isle of Wight, I decided on the Portsmouth route as the most suitable. The cattle barge is timed to leave The Point, Portsmouth Harbour, at 2p.m., and cars are expected to be on board at 1.30. Unexpected delays, traffic for instance, occurred, the boat had gone, and I was cheerfully informed on the quay that the boat would start 'tomorrow.'

A way out of the difficulty had to found, so I called on the traffic superintendent of the joint railways at Portsmouth town station, and asked that as a favour the car might be ferried across on a passenger steamer. After some demur, consent was given, but allusion was made to a previous case in which the Superintendent had heard of difficulties on Ryde Pier after disembarkation. I accepted the risk and drove off to the Harbour station while instructions for the disposal of the car were telephoned on.

The next step was payment of 20s (£1.00) and signature on a paper indemnifying the railway company from liability. The car was pushed on to the upper deck of the steamer without difficulty, and the skipper was glad of a hint to spread a tarpaulin under it, and save his spotless decks from oil. On arrival at Ryde Pier the fun began. The tide was high, and the deck towered above the level of the pier. It was necessary to lower the car down the planks with ropes, the gradient seemed quite 1 in 3. This was safely accomplished after some minutes delay to the steamer.

Arrived at 'pierra firma' all that seemed necessary was to drive down the length of the pier on to Ryde Esplanade. Not at all. The toll-gate collector of the pier promenade declined to allow the car to leave the pier head. The Manager was sent for, and asserted that the gates at the shore end would not be wide enough to allow egress to the car. The gates at the pier head would have admitted a pantechnicon. The width of my small car was only 4ft 8 inches and I asked to be allowed to drive down and try. Permission for this was refused. It then transpired that some weeks before a large car had been similarly disembarked at the pier head, and on reaching the pier gates they were just too narrow for it to pass out. The pier officials then overcame the difficulty by obtaining planks, and with considerable trouble passed the car down on to the electric tramline and up again beyond the gate. The owner seems to have regarded their labours as all in a day's work, and having paid the legal toll of 6d departed. Small wonder that motorcars were unpopular with the Ryde Pier officials.

Argument and persuasion being useless, the only way off the pier was by train. Those who know the Isle of Wight and its railways will understand what a novelty it was to the railway company to carry a motor-car. The Isle of Wight Railway has a carriage truck. It had to traced and ordered to Ryde Pier head. At length it arrived, but of course it was designed, as most carriage trucks are, for end loading in a carriage dock. To get the car over its high sides the bookstall tables had to be commandeered from their trestles and, with the aid of most of the Isle of Wight Railways staff, the car was finally deposited on its truck and attached to the rear of the train. In this ignominious manner it travelled as far as St. John's Road station, little more than a mile. There it spent an hour on its truck waiting for an engine to shunt it into the carriage dock. The engine had to be fetched from a train at a neighbouring station - a peculiarity of Isle of Wight traffic.

Finally the car was driven out of the station yard at 6.30p.m.. The time occupied from Ryde Pier head to Ryde town was three hours, the distance 1fi miles. The cost of the journey, including tips, was 35s (£1.75p). The cost of the carriage truck for the lfi mile journey was 7s6d (37p); and as the weight of the car was less than half a ton, the rate per ton-mile should make the mouth of any traffic manager duly water. On the whole, not withstanding the courtesy of the railway officials on both sides of the water, the journey by this means is not be recommended. Certainly not to those of an impatient temperament.

Isle of Wight Observer, 23 March 1903

The Village Bus

Mr Robert Smith, Alverstone
We also had a bus run through the village in the 1920s by one Cyril Cooke. His first bus was a model 'T Ford, with a dozen seats or less and he made two trips to Sandown and one to Newport daily. Often there were as many standing as sitting and I remember on a trip to Mersley Down they had to get out and push the old bus to help the gears. Several times he would reverse all the way up the Shute in order to engage the lower gear. What a great service he delivered right to the door and most times left the item in the kitchen while the passengers sat and waited. He would run a very late bus for Regatta night and no-one was ever left behind.

Newchurch Remembered, *Newchurch Women's Institute (1988)*

9 · AGRICULTURE

Farming has always been at the heart of Island life and we are fortunate that its geology has given us a land that has for centuries produced two elements of successful farming, corn and sheep. The rich greensands in the centre and south of the Island produced wheat in abundance and the miles of open downland kept the other necessary partner, the sheep who manured the ground, and gave, too, an additional crop in their valuable fleeces. The progress of local agriculture has been recorded from medieval times to the present, showing the gradual development of farming over the centuries.

Medieval Rabbits

The Isle of Wight is included in those places where rabbits are first recorded. They are not native animals but were introduced by the Normans and the first signs of them are noted in islands off the southern coasts in the 12th century. The Island rabbits were close behind them.

The next early document to mention the presence of rabbits in Britain is an account of 1225 for the manor of Bowcombe in the Isle of Wight. Here among the expenses we find the wages of the keeper of the conies and among the receipts the sale of two hundred rabbit skins . . .

That rabbits were readily available in considerable quantities is clear from the royal demand of 7 November 1243 to take for the king 100 rabbits in the Isle of Wight and send them to Westminster by 19 November. Again the keeper of the lands of the late Baldwin de Insula was ordered on 16 December 1248, to take 100 rabbits from these lands for the king and send them to Westminster by Christmas Eve.

Poaching then as now, had its attractions and its devotees, while owners were out to defend their warrens. On Tuesday 23 November, a rabbit-hunting party consisting of Thomas Smythe, Roger Hegham and John atte Nore came about midnight to the property of Geoffrey Roukle in the tithing of Brook. They were armed with bows and arrows, while Thomas Smythe was carrying a shield. They were busy laying out their nets and were using ferrets to drive out the rabbits, when they caught sight of the warreners, John Thornor and Richard Knoll. Thereupon the rabbiters fired at the keepers with their arrows intending to kill them. In self-defence the keepers returned the fire. John Thornor wounded Thomas Smythe in the head, on the left side of the forehead, from which he died.'

S.F. *Hockey*, Insula Vecta, (*1982*)

A 'Champion' Village

In 1630 the estate of the Barrington family in the Isle of Wight was surveyed following the death of Sir Francis Barrington. John Harrison, the surveyor, kept detailed accounts and his description of Brighstone shows a thriving community still farming in open fields on each side of the village.

On 6 July Harrison wrote to Lady Joan Barrington, 'I go to Brixton [Brighstone] w[i]ch lyeth in such littele pclls(parcels) of land and intermixt with so many severall lands of other men that I feare I shall be a greate while about it.' He left Swainston on 29 July to stay with Joan Baker, the miller, at Shate Place, one of the most comfortable houses in Brighstone. When Harrison topped the downs between Calbourne and Brighstone he saw below him a flat plain open to the cliffs and sea on the south coast, open 'champion' country, unhedged and treeless. In the centre of this manor was Brighstone, a thriving community which rightly called itself a township. Farmhouses and cottages radiated from the church, there were three shops entered in the survey and a large public building the Church House, within which was the school. Near the village to the south was the mill and beyond the mill, extending to Sutton, was a district of isolated farms, most with old farmhouses, which formed a community of its own. A smaller manor, Waytes Court, was also part of Brighstone, the manor house lying less than a mile south of the church. It was the tenants of Alexander Wayte, the lord of the manor, whose lands were 'intermixt' with those of Swainston. Berrybarn the ancient manor house of Brighstone, stood within the village, a short distance south of the church.

. . . Harrison saw that there were no trees or copses to be valued; in common with all champion farming areas the woodland had long since disappeared. The tenants were expected to plant six new trees each year and he instructed the bailiff to find out how many were planted and to encourage tenants to plant each year.

Visually the most dramatic features of the landscape were the open fields on each side of the village, with their pasture and arable blocks and strips ; Westfield lying between the centre of the village to below Brighstone and Calbourne downs, Ugdon or Uggaton field, also on the west of the village, and the great East field. This ran from the edge of the village eastwards almost to Limerston, south to Thorne Place at the east and back to Marsh Place at the west, a great open area of farmland.

Johanna Jones, 'The 1630 Survey of Swainston – farm buildings and farmlands', (2003)

Farmers have a long-standing reputation for grumbling. John Hall's letters of the 1660s are no exception, covering everything from the weather to taxes.

John Hall 31 August 1666
the price of corn in the Island is very low, and like to be lower, and so likewise are all commodities that farmers have to sell. Here hath been very much dry weather this great while, insomuch that many complain for want of water as well as grass for their cattle.

4 January 1668
wheat and barley are both very low in price here – the best wheat not exceeding 3/-and barley 2/3d the bushel.

27 October 1668

I have the worst crop of wheat that I ever had, and I think my neighbours is not much better. I would gladly take 4d the pound for butter and lfid a pound for cheese, for all that is made this year . . . wool, which you write in yours of Sept. 7th is in Norfolk advanced from 14/- to 24/-, I do not hear that here hath been offered or given above 22/- per todd for the best wool in this Island, which is but a small advance. I confess I see no great reason for it, unless it be the scarcity of money, and the high taxes here.

John Hall, Letters *(Isle of Wight County Record Office)*

Sowing Wheat and making Ricks, 1700

Edward Lisle, a landowner with a keen interest in agriculture, lived in Crux Easton, north Hampshire, but held land in the Isle of Wight. His conversations with his tenants and his own observation show local conditions governed the planting of wheat.

Dec. 19 1700 I saw ground of farmer Farthing [Appleford] in the Isle of Wight sown to wheat. I also saw some other persons sowing then; I thought it very late, and asked the farmer about it. He said, that in their country (the winter being milder than with us at Crux Easton) if sandy and poorish land be sown early, it will have spent its strength on the halm, or green wheat, before the spring and summer comes, and will not be able to maintain the crop.

The sheaves were set with ears uppermost in the first circle and so on in every rundle, till at length it draws into a point; and then a sheaf is opened and turned with the ears downwards . . . for an ear turned downwards will not grow, nor take wet by half a year's wet weather, and the bottom of the sheaf being broader than the top, every uppermost circle hangs over the sheaves of the undermost circle, like the eaves of a house . . . Farmer Miles says, that in that fashion without thatching, they make wheat ricks in the Isle of Wight.

Edward Lisle, Observations in Husbandry *2nd. ed. 1757*

A Survey of Farming 1795

The number of sheep annually shorn is computed to amount to forty thousand. In the year 1793, five thousand lambs were sold to the London butchers alone. The stock usually kept on the farms consists of sheep, cows, and horses; oxen are rare, what few there are, the farmers generally feed with straw and hay, and work them as horses.

The cows are mostly of the Devon, breed, though blended with other sorts. The farmers also make a point of having a few Alderney cows in their dairies, which they think produce a better and sweeter butter than would be made without their milk. These little animals are extremely profitable, some of them giving to the dairy, during part of the summer, nine and ten pounds of butter per week. The horses are of different breeds, but in general large. The draught-horses are fine animals, and kept in excellent order. The *hogs* are of a breed, I believe, peculiar to the island. They are large and tall, marked with black spots, and have very deep sides; their bacon is excellent.

The dairies produce, in considerable quantities, a particular kind of skim-milk cheese, emphatically called the *Isle of Wight rock*. It is extremely hard; can scarcely be cut by a hatchet or saw; is to be masticated only by the firmest teeth; and digested only by the strongest stomachs. The grains chiefly cultivated here are, wheat, barley oats, pease, and beans. In the neighbourhood of the sea, the farmers prefer the *old white strawed wheat*, for the sensible reason of its being less liable than any other kind to be injured by high winds and tempestuous weather. On the North part of the island, the red-strawed wheat is usually sown; as well as in all the wet, poor lands, because it is supposed to *run more to straw* than any other kind, and of course enables the farmer to provide more fodder for his cattle in the winter . . .

The grain is in general broadcast, though some farmers have adopted the drilling system for wheat, barley, and pease, which is found to succeed well in the free, light sandy soils . . . The system of *fallows*, both summer and winter, is pretty generally followed throughout the island; nor will many of the farmers hear of a contrary practice.

Their manures are chiefly chalk and dung arising from the farm-yard which after lying for some time in a heap, is mixed with earth. Chalk is also much used. They put about one hundred bushels of it upon an acre, which continue to operate beneficially for fourteen or fifteen years.

Rev. Richard Warner, The History of the Isle of Wight, (*1795*)

A Victorian 'Improver'

By the 1860s landowners who could afford to do so were making radical changes to farming.

George Young, Esq. purchased four years since, 730 acres of land at Ashey. It was at the time of purchase, a wilderness of trees, bushes, and crooked fences, under water and without roads, almost in a state of nature. Mr. Young has grubbed 150 acres of oak coppice, and has put, or is putting, it under cultivation. He has made roads, straightened the fences, and thrown his fields together for the steam plough.

He has made his own bricks and pipes of the clay on the property, erected sawing machinery, and himself superintended the erection of the whole. Liberal applications of farmyard and artificial manures are made. Last year 14 tons of guano, and 20 tons of Lawes's superphosphates, were used, beside all the dung made at home and what the town of Ryde could supply. Within the last three years 1900 tons of dung have been bought, in Ryde, and its neighbourhood.

Journal of the Royal Agricultural Society of England, (*1861*)

A Late Victorian Farm

In the 1890s a farm of any size had horses, cattle sheep, pigs, poultry and a dairy. Consequently many more workers were employed. Usually a carter, carter's mate, a head cowman whose wife often worked in the dairy, and a second cowman. There was a shepherd and a man who could thatch ricks, as well as do the hedging and ditching. Finally there was a boy who carried milk around the village and looked after the poultry. During busy times extra hands were needed – gangs of men toured around to shear the sheep and help with turnip hoeing.

On one farm I knew in my childhood (Waytes Court), there was no main water. Drinking water was fetched from a spring by an old man and brought to the house in two buckets slung on a yoke across his shoulders. The water was then put into large earthenware containers which contained a filter.

There were many lovely sights in the country which have disappeared now. Anyone who has seen a row of men bending in unison to cut ripe corn, and has heard the swishing of their scythes as they cut will understand what I mean. What lovelier sight than a team of heavy shire horses, all glorious with shining coats, washed and brushed tails and manes, with strings of brasses on their harness. The carters took pride in the stables and hung records of prizes on the beams.

Over one stable there was a primitive sort of bedroom known as the Carter's Chamber which might be used by one of the unmarried men.

A periodic visitor was the old Bagman. Before the corn was threshed the bags had to be overhauled and mended, and the old man travelled round doing this work. He used to be given meals in the old brewhouse and sometimes slept in one of the old stables.

At the end of a hot day's work during the haymaking or harvest, the men came into the back court and were given a pint of beer. There was always a cask in the cellar and a familiar sight in the kitchen was a row of pint cups hanging on the old wooden dresser.

Mabel Roach, Brighstone Village, Isle of Wight *(2004)*

A Farm Worker in 1926

Robert Cassell left school in 1926 just before his fourteenth birthday and went to work at Seaview Dairy, near Compton. He was paid 9s (45p) a week for general farm work. 'I had fifteen cows to look after, three horses and about fifteen pigs. They all had to be fed and looked after. The horses names were Bird and Diamond . . . the pony's name was Joe. The cows were called names like Primrose and Cherry – flower names mostly. Some of the cows were Frisian but most of them was Guernseys. They give better milk for butter making although not quite as good as Jerseys. There would only be about ten or eleven cows in milk at a time and I milked them by hand. Each cow would take about ten minutes at the outside in summer time when their udders were nice and big. We would start milking at half past six in the morning. A third of the cows we had I reared from calves.

I had a two and a half mile walk to work so in the winter it was well and truly dark. I would have a candle in a lantern or a hurricane lantern – you really wanted another to see that one. In the summer when I got there, I would go and bring in the cows but in winter they would have already been in the stable. Before starting milking you had to clean them up a bit. They was milked into a pail. The milk was then taken to a separator where you turned a handle and the skim milk came out one side and the cream the other. The cream was for butter making and most of the skim was fed to the little pigs who went crazy for it . . .

After milking I used to take the skimmed milk out to mix up with the pigs' food and feed the pigs. Then at nine o'clock it was time for what we called 'nammet', that's the Isle of Wight word for elevenses or refreshments. After that I would clean out the stables, wash them down you know ready for the cows to come back in the afternoon. There was always lots of other things to do, feeding and looking after the horses, cleaning the dirt off the mangels, putting them in a machine that sliced them up when I turned a handle. Well that took almost a day. The mangels were for the cows with a bit of meal on top of them. They mostly had that in the winter. In the summer the cows had plenty of grass.

Robert Cassell, ed. Dina Broughton, An Eventful Life, (*1997*)

An Agricultural Survey 1933

In 1933 a camp for schoolboys was set up in Chale. The boys, aged between 12 and 14 were taking part in an agricultural survey, one of the first of its kind. They went out in pairs to visit farms armed with a set of questions which the farmers had to answer while the boys were there. Ninety three farms were recorded and they give a revealing view of rural life at that time.

'. . . milk trains yearly carry over 500,000 gallons to Ryde for Portsmouth. The number of cars, lorries and buses has increased to such an extent that the narrow Isle of Wight roads have their own traffic problems, one-way traffic for heavy vehicles being the rule over several stretches of rural road way.

In the north milk is sent to the mainland; but in the south the more difficult communications results in the bulk being made into butter and the Isle of Wight has one of the largest butter outputs as it has the largest pig population in England today (per 1000 acres crops and grass).

Market gardening has made little headway, mainly on account of the shortage of labour in the summer. Neither casual men for heavy work nor women for picking and packing are obtainable – both are offered higher wages in the distributive trades catering for summer visitors. There is a steady drift of labour to the towns, where work is easier and better paid. Some workers find their way back to the land, but shepherds

are born and bred, and gaps in the ranks of old men are not being filled.
L.R. Wood 'Agricultural Survey' Geography, vol. 18, 1933

The Farmer's Wife

When my husband and I farmed Lower Knighton Farm about 1934 onwards my day was something like this. Get up at six thirty a.m. and have a cup of tea made by boiling a kettle of water on a double-burner oil stove. Then light the copper fire in the old brewhouse to get water hot for use in the dairy and cow-stable. While this was heating up the big range fire was lit (we had to use one hundred weight of coal to get this hot enough for roasting and baking) and this was given up after a time in favour of a three-burner oil stove and double oven . . . Until we left in 1948 . . . there was no gas or electricity and water was obtained from a pump just outside the back door which was fed from the well. We could get extra cold water from the well close to the old Mill House down the road. This water was excellent for washing the butter after churning and before it was lightly salted, then rolled many times to get the whey from it, then weighed into half-pound pats and shaped with a cow or a rose pattern on top. I was paid an extra halfpenny a pound for making this. The most I made in a week (Tuesday and Friday being butter-making days) was approximately two hundred and fifty pounds .
. . After milking was finished – breakfast. In summertime I would feed all the poultry, chickens, ducks and geese before breakfast, but after breakfast in winter . . . I was paid one penny a dozen for washing the eggs for sale and allowed a chicken at Christmas. My milk allowance was one pint a day. We paid no rent as we lived in the farmhouse and our wages for two was £1.10.0 (£1.50). This went up to £2.10.0 when our first son was born.

. . . to help out with fuel and time, I had a large box which I lined with several layers of newspapers, then a thick layer of straw, then hay and this was covered with a thick blanket. This was my hay-box. To use it I would cook porridge on the stove, then it was put in the box (the lid lined as the box); and it was ready piping hot for breakfast next day. Rabbit stew, with onions, carrots, turnips, potatoes and dumplings was done this way as well – really lovely.

Mrs Ivy Welstead, Newchurch Remembered, *Newchurch Women's Institute (1988)*

10 · WORK-FOLK AND THE POOR

A House of Industry

An advertisement placed in the Salisbury Journal *in October 1770 was probably the most important announcement made in the Island during the eighteenth century. It was the first indication that the care of the poor was to pass from the individual parishes to a central administration in Newport. This was achieved despite opposition, thirteen of the thirty parishes opposing the private act of parliament, but the power of the gentry and clergy prevailed and an Act for establishing a workhouse, or House of Industry, in the Isle of Wight received Royal Assent on 8 May 1771.*

Sept. 28 1770
Whereas a proposal has been made to consolidate the rates or assessments made for the relief of the poor of the several parishes of the Isle of Wight, and to institute one or more houses of industry, for the maintenance of the poor in general of the said Island, and at a meeting of the committee for the purpose aforesaid, held at the Sun Inn, in Newport this day, it was resolved.

That an abstract be made of an act of parliament for the better relief and employment of the poor in the hundred of Samford, in the county of Suffolk, for the consideration of the committe, in order to settle a plan, to be pursued in this Island: such an act being thought a proper groundwork for the intended institution, and that twelve copies of the said act of parliament be purchased for the use of the committee.

That letters be written by the Secretary to the ministers of the several parishes in the Island, requesting them to send accounts to the committee of the number of poor maintained in their several parishes: and also the gross amount of the rates granted for the relief of the poor of such parishes for the last seven years . . .

That a clause be inserted in the act of parliament for vesting the several houses and lands given to the several parishes in the Island for the immediate relief of the poor of such parishes, in trustees under the act, to be sold for the purpose of building the houses of industry . . .

By order of
Sir William Oglander, Bart
John Eames
Nash Grose   Esqurs
James Worsley
Edward Worsley
Rev. L. Troughear Holmes

Rev. Dr. Jefferson
Rev. Dr. Walker
Rev. Mr. Fisher
Rev. Mr. Shan
Rev. Mr. Dickenson

Richard Clarke, Secretary

A single House of Industry, red-brick and vast, stood on the empty heath of Parkhurst Forest, just outside Newport on the road to Cowes. It was the largest rural workhouse in the kingdom, housing six hundred inmates, and could be pointed out with pride to visitors.

> We must not pass unnoticed by,
> The Spacious House of Industry;
> A work which Policy approves,
> Religion owns and mercy loves;
> Snatched from some vulgar Overseer,
> Most ignorant and most severe,
> Here feeble poverty has found,
> A Sanctuary to guard her round;
> To yield each aid and end her days
> In comfort and in pious praise,
> Here the young race of casual birth,

Who would be outcasts on the earth,
Bred to no learning, taught to shun
No vice, but swift to ruin run,
Meet blessed Instructions' cheering ray
Their God to serve and Man obey . . .

William Smart, A Rumble from Newport to Cowes (1782)

A Scandal in the School

The voices of the poor, speaking for themselves, are rarely heard, but in 1839 a literate pauper who assisted in the workhouse boys' school was bold enough to write to the Chairman of the Guardians, the Reverend Walton White, concerning the conditions in the school, and by his intervention brought about an improvement. He also showed that he had a wider understanding of what education was than was usual in those days.

Revd. Sir,

Two gentlemen looked over the school last week one of them I think Captn Farrington observed that the Boys ought to go out four times a week knowing as I do that the Boys do not go out scarcely once a week I wrote to Captn Farrington about it Yesterday being a half Holyday the Schoolmaster sent word to the Governor to know if he should take the Boys out the Governor sent back an answer that he should do so this very young schoolmaster instead of doing as ordered never took the Boys out – but went out himself the Governor is ignorant of the practice of this young man poor Boys they want a little fresh air now and then it would make them grow

A little boy Clarke by name a bad boy was punished most severely four weeks ago he ran away but is here now and has had clogs on since and is not suffered to play with the Boys this hurt his spirits so much that he yesterday tried to strangle himself and probably would have done it had he not been prevented by Simmonds and Dash two Boys.

The Schoolmaster took no notice of the circumstances surely the Boy ought to be talked to or put under some restraint I have no vindictive feelings against the young Man but he ought to be taught that there are other Qualities wanted besides mere Reading, Writing and Arithmetic to constitute a good Schoolmaster

I remain Revd Sir, Your humble Servant, W. Tyrrell

A Workhouse Report

Report of the Committee appointed to examine the state of the Schools in the House of Industry.

The girls' school received a good report, except that the National system should be carried out as far as possible and that some rewards should be distributed by the Chaplain at the monthly examinations.

With regard to the Boys School they likewise recommend that the National system should be more effectually carried out and for this purpose rewards should be in the like manner distributed at the monthly examinations.

That the Chaplain be requested to hold such monthly examinations of the separate classes and to visit the School occasionally at other times to see the National system is carried on and superintend its working.

That henceforth no Boys shall be withdrawn during school hours for any purpose and that the working class shall only be employed in learning any work, business or trade, out of School hours – particularly on the two half holidays in the week.

That the Boys have an improved Dietary according to a scale annexed – and to be supplied with 2 suits of clothing and stockings made in the House – and with some materials for play and recreation suitable to their condition.

That a respectable man be employed under the Master to assist him occasionally in the School during School hours and at all other times to be with the Boys to superintend their conduct and watch their morals and habits.

That a respectable woman be employed to take care of the Boys' bedding, clothing and linen & the apartments belonging to the School with such assistance from the women in the House as has hitherto been usual.

House of Industry May 29, 1839, R.W. White, Chairman
Isle of Wight Record Office, Newport

In 1822 Valentine Gray, a ten year old climbing boy was found dead in an out-building of his master's house in Pyle Street, Newport. He had been severely beaten and died from a blow to his head. His master was sentenced to one year in prison for manslaughter, although there is no evidence that he ever served his sentence. The exposure of such cruelty in their own community produced an immediate reaction and a public subscription raised money for a simple monument to Valentine Gray, 'the little sweep'. Valentine Gray was the inspiration for this poem, when the climbing boy visits a seventeenth century manor house at Shorwell.

The Sweepboy at Northcourt

A better class of chimney – wide
unlike the reeky flues of Newport

his master takes him to the house
on blackened cart behind the farty nag

never saw a place like this, nor the tired
but well- dressed lady opening the door

(he later sees her scrubbing in the kitchen)
rooms as big as he imagines inside churches are

cannot believe his nine year eyes, red-rimmed
and cinder scraped - then the cuff and boot up backside

scrambles, curses, scrapes re-open, ulcers bleed
as usual, rooks and daws above remote as heaven

after a gulp of beer, master pockets coin
claims he feeds the boy too well - look how

he grows, not long left for him the chimney way.
Nights under the table with his beetle friends

dreams of airy rooms soon overwhelmed
by stacks and rubble, rough cast brick

droppings from old birds' nests, the ever-itch
of soot, one dream (hopelessly above his station)

that he might rise to stable boy when
too large to scramble chimneys.

Robin Ford, South *(2004) (poetry collection)*

Arson was one way the poor expressed their frustrations. It continued intermittently over many years and was often accompanied by threatening notices, such as this posted on the door of St Thomas's Church, Newport, in 1804.

A Cousen for the farmers and those that was the incegation of the unecesary rise upon flower and Bread we do hearby declare and give public notice that if you dont lore the price as before we will put fire to every Wheat Rick within our Reach For we think it necesary that the rich should starve as well as the poor and so you may depend on this as truth.
Hampshire Telegraph, 25 *April*, (1804)

A letter sent in November 1830 to Dean Wood, Dean of Ely, and a notorious absentee rector of Freshwater.

For the last 20 years wee have been in a Starving Condition to maintain your dam Pride.

What we have done now is Soar against our Will but your hart is so hard as the hart of Pharo . . . So now as for this fire you must not take it as a front [an affront] for if you hadent been Deserving it wee should not have dont As for you my Ould frend you dident happen to be hear if that you had been rosted I fear and if it had been so how the farmers would lagh to see the old Pasen rosted at last . . .

As for this litel fire . . . Dont be alarmed it will be a damd deal wors when we Burn down your barn. . . .
E.P. Thompson, The Making of the English Working Class, (1968)

The Macnamara Almshouses, Cowes

This small group of twelve Almshouses was built in 1881 by the Rev. Thomas Macnamara in memory of his parents. Here twelve poor women lived rent free with a small pension, each with a single room and a scullery. Those who lived on the ground floor lost a little privacy as the stairs to the upper floor rooms had to rise from their sculleries. Rules II and III reflect the ways in which poor women earned a little money when they were living independently.

Rules

I. The Alms Women shall be clean in Person and Attire ; and their Rooms shall be kept clean and neat.

II. Needlework may be taken, but no Washing or Ironing except their own shall be done on the premises; and Clothes shall not be hung out to dry in the Garden in Front of the Houses; and no kind of work shall be undertaken – unless by special permission – for other Persons, necessitating absence from home at night-

III. No lodger shall be received; and Children shall not be permitted to reside with any of the Inmates.

IV. The Alms Women shall be kind and helpful to one another, and temperate in their habits.

V. They shall, if well and able, always attend the Public Worship of Almighty God on the LORD'S DAY, and at such other times as may be convenient to them.

VI. The Trustees have power to demand possession of the rooms on giving a month's notice to any Inmate who breaks the Rules.

VII. A copy of these rules shall be displayed in every Almshouse.

Held by St Mary's Church, Cowes.

The Hermit of Chale

Isaac Sheath was clearly very eccentric, but such an individual can live a reasonably happy life in a community where he is recognized and accepted. This he managed to do for most of his life, living in a mud hut he had made for himself. It was a rectangular room cut into the bank, the walls entirely of earth, with a rough thatch roof to protect them from rain. The chimney was set opposite the door, the most practical place for a stove. Any material that came to hand was put to good use from strong posts discarded from grander houses to packing cases. The planking on one side of his door was stencilled 'Tate and Sons Cube Sugar'. At the end of his life he was forced to move as new housing legislation made his home 'unfit for human habitation'.

The death occurred in the infirmary at Parkhurst on Sunday of Mr Isaac Sheath, familiar to many Islanders and visitors as 'The hermit of Chale-green.' The deceased, whose age is officially given as 75, but who was believed to be nearly 80, was of very eccentric habits, which led him to live alone for some 30 years in a mud hut he had built on a waste piece of land at North-grounds, Chale, his occupancy of which came to an end last year, when the Rural District Council, under the new housing legislation, had his primitive dwelling condemned as unfit for human habitation, and Sheath was removed to the Workhouse.

He was a native of Chale-green, belonged to a farm labourer's family, and his lack of energy and mental capacity in his youth led to domestic differences at home. After the death of his mother he went into lodgings, but these he eventually deserted for his roadside hut, where he was a familiar figure to passers-by, coaching parties and others, who took great and often kindly interest in him, and he received many small monetary gifts, but never thought of saving up for the winter, when he had to rely on parish relief and the hospitality of a few friends in Chale-green.

With good reason he regarded Mr. J. H. Brown, C.C. and Mrs. Brown of Chale-green, as his best friends, and to Mr. Brown he went with all his troubles, which arose principally from boys tormenting him by pulling down the chimney pot, throwing stones down the chimney, and otherwise invading his humble abode.

The Rector of Chale and his wife were also very good to him and in the winter provided him with coal, evidence of the arrival of which was afforded by his begrimed face and hands.

Several years ago two residents in the parish kindly match-boarded his hut inside to make it more comfortable, and Sheath showed his appreciation by gradually stripping off the boards to save himself the trouble of collecting firewood; a mattress, table, and chair also given him had a like fate. He was of a sympathetic disposition and fond of children.

He was visited in his last illness by Mrs. J.H. Brown and others and stated that he was well cared for and comfortable, though he still had a longing for the free open-air life of bygone years.

When the sanitary inspector of the Rural District Council condemned Sheath's hut and told him it must be pulled down the hermit replied, 'Sooner than they should do that I will burn it down,' and those who were superintending his removal next day saw the hut in flames on their approach.

Isle of Wight County Press, *24th February* (1912)

II · SMUGGLING

The high days of smuggling were in the eighteenth and early nineteenth centuries when heavy duties on imported goods made the dangers of smuggling worthwhile to the seamen in the Island. The excise men had enormous difficulties in controlling smuggling, and it was only when they had fast and well-armed boats in the early nineteenth century that endemic smuggling in the Island was brought to an end.

William Arnold

For a long period Cowes was in charge of one of the ablest men in the service, Mr. William Arnold, father of the celebrated Head Master of Rugby. Arnold came from a family already settled into the Excise service in which his father and his only uncle both served. He began his work on 30 September 1777 but it was cut short by his sudden and unexpected death on 3 March 1801. His letters give a lively and authoritative account of smuggling around the Island at the end of the eighteenth century.

Arnold to the Board of Customs Oct. 1783

We beg leave to report that within the last three years smuggling has increased upon this coast to an alarming degree. Illicit trade is principally carried on in large armed cutters or luggers from two to three hundred tons burthen, with which the Revenue cutters are not able to contend. It is no unusual thing for them to land their goods in open day under protection of their guns, sometimes in sight of Revenue cutters whom they will not suffer to come near or board them. The war [of American Independence] gave a sanction to the arming of these vessels, as the masters took out commissions as privateers, tho' in fact they followed no other trade than smuggling Now the war is over they continue their illicit practices.

If they sell at sea to small coasting vessels or boats, the price of a 4 gallon cask is about half a guinea; if landed on shore between Hurst and Christchurch under the protection of their guns and put into quiet possession of the land smugglers, 14/- (78p) or 15/- a cask; if brought within the Isle of Wight, to Langstone or Portsmouth, the price advances to a guinea a cask.'

The First Swan Cutter

Arnold to John Delafield, his-brother-in-law. I. of Wight 2 Dec. 1783
Dear Johnny,

. . . In my last [letter] I told you the hopes I had of success from my *Swan* cutter which was just commissioned, but alas all our hopes are fled by the unfortunate loss of the vessel in a violent gale of wind the 14 November, between the Needles and Hurst. It is indeed a heavy blow upon me; the outfit, purchase &c. stood in between £800 and £900. I held a moiety, Joe a quarter and the commander a quarter. What is saved from the wreck I suppose will not produce £40, so that we call it a total loss.

The Second Swan

'The contract with the Commissioners for the new 90-ton cutter was signed in March, 1784, and in April Arnold had the pleasure of seeing her in Cowes harbour. She was named *Swan* after the last one.

Soon after the new cutter arrived from the Thames, the ten little six-pounder guns, which Sarmon had recovered from the shingle at Hurst, were peeping through her ports. The heavy four-oared jolly-boat, saved from the wreck, was hoisted on board. At her peak flew the blue

Customs ensign with its symbolic badge – the portcullis of a castle – in the fly. Before opening fire on a smuggling vessel, she was required by law to hoist this ensign and a masthead pennant of similar design, and to fire a warning gun.

The appointments of George Sarmon as commander, and of the mate, had been made out by the Commissioners of Customs on Arnold's recommendation. They also sent documents called 'deputations' for the commander, mate, and for one of the mariners, called the 'deputy mariner'. No search or seizure could be made except in the presence of one of these three. Twenty one local mariners were engaged for the crew.

These typically English cutters were always clinker built, this method of lapped planking, handed down from the Norsemen, being considered more suitable for rough and tumble work than the smooth-sided carvel fashion more commonly used by foreign boat builders. Those for the Customs service, being required to keep to sea for long periods in all weathers, had to be more stoutly built than the smugglers' vessels that could pick and choose weather for short runs. Yet in spite of this, the Revenue craft required if possible more speed than the lightly built smugglers . . .

Rear-Admiral D. Foster, At War With The Smugglers, (1970)

Smuggling at Bembridge

Situated as it was, with the old Brading Haven and all its creeks close by, it goes without saying that many a good cargo of contraband found its way into Bembridge, but the game was always carried on as a contest of brains and skill between the smugglers and the Revenue Authorities, and it never seems to have been disgraced by those outrages which in some other parts of the country shocked and disgusted everyone.

The chief traffic used to be brandy and tobacco, which were usually procured from Cherbourg and Barfleur, and the goods were made up in light oak tubs called ankers, each holding 10 gallons, and half ankers of 5 gallon capacity. These tubs were of light weight and well made, so that they could be submerged under the sea for several days, if necessary, without their contents getting damaged.

The duty in England on brandy at the busiest time of smuggling, i.e., from 1825 to 1840, used to be thirty-two shillings per gallon, so that anyone who could successfully run over in his boat a crop of 100 tubs, was assured of a good profit after selling the brandy to the publicans at a price far below that at which liquor, which had honestly paid its duty could be sold.

Very large profits also were made on tea and tobacco, for the duty on the former was as high as four shillings a pound, and that on tobacco only a little less. Here, then, is the key to the popularity and universal prevalence of smuggling. Times were often hard, and wages low, in those days, but a dashing young chap could soon make a few hundred pounds, and the scantily paid farm labourer was naturally pleased to earn a guinea for a few hours work at night in assisting a run.

The penalties were severe it is true if caught – imprisonment, or five years service on a 'man-o'-war – which was often worse than the former, but frequently the magistrate before whom they were brought, was if not an actual smuggler, at any rate in sympathy with them, and both he and his wife were pretty sure to be users and customers of run goods; brandy and tobacco for the former, and silks, laces and brocades for the latter, so small wonder was that if a legal point could be strained or a quibble brought in, the prisoners were dismissed with a caution . . .

The system of smuggling . . . most in use at Bembridge was known as 'rafting in'. A vessel would sail over from France, and carefully time her arrival, and her day, so that just after dusk she would be Under Tyne with a strong flood tide running into the harbour. The tubs would then all be tied together so as to form an elongated raft, and they were so weighted with iron plates or stones that they were well under water and out of sight.

All night long during the 'darks', i.e. when there was no moon, a watch boat would be anchored just in the middle of the mouth of the Harbour so the problem was, how to get the raft in without the lookout seeing it.

One well known Bembridge man, old S., used to accomplish this by floating himself with only his nose and mouth above the water and holding in his hand a light rope attached to the tubs. As soon as the tide had carried him and his freight well inside the Harbour he would, by swimming and wading, gradually edge up to one of the beaches, where helping hands were waiting to rush the tubs inland, each man carrying two slung together, one on his back, and one on his breast, his head hung between the two rope slings which rested on his shoulders.

. . . For many years a well-known old lady at Bembridge used to carry out a very thriving business by ostensibly going round selling fish, but also selling brandy to any customer who was in the know, and whom she could trust. And active and well set-up she was, with a very buxom figure, who thought nothing of walking into Ryde and back with her basket of fish. The Excise people had long been on her track, knowing that she sold something more than her fish, but they could never get proofs. At last one day she was stopped when near Ryde by one of the Riding officers, who declared that she must come over to Portsmouth with him to be searched, for there were no female searchers in the Island.

There was, of course, no refusing such an order, so the two proceeded to Ryde Pier to take the steamer across, but whilst awaiting its arrival alongside, the old lady retired behind one of the sheds for a short time, and on re-appearing the Riding officer could scarcely believe his eyes, for, in place of the well-known figure, a somewhat gaunt woman met his gaze, who jeeringly asked him when the boat would be starting. The brandy, which had been concealed about her person in various bladders, had been dropped into the Solent, so there was now no evidence at all, and the disconsolate officer postponed his trip across, and returned to Bembridge.

Ernest du Boulay, Bembridge Past and Present, *(1911)*

A Smuggling Tale from Niton

My favourite smuggling story comes from W.H. Long's Dialect of the Isle of Wight *where it illustrates the word 'Voreright' – blundering, headstrong, regardless of consequences.*

Aye, they deed use to do a lot o' smugglen about here fifty or sixty years agoo, when I was a bwoy. I've heerd my father zay, one time dree or vower on 'em, wi tubs and bags o' tay, got ver' near took by the Customs House officers, but they managed to git off the shore and into the churchyard at Niton; but zome o' the officers had slipped round another road, and prid near penned 'em in all zides. They must have thought 'twas a gooser [an upshot or end of everything] wi' 'em, but one on 'em, a terbul voreright feller, called Mussel, zays: 'Come on, mayets, I be darned if I won't be upzides wi' they fellers; zoo they prised up the stoan on one o' they gurt brick tombs theres there, and got inside, tubs and all, and bid quiet. Cooase the officers lost 'em, and couldn't think where the deuce they was gone to, and aater serchen about a bit they went away.

Zoon aaterwards, jest as 'twas gitten daylight, my father was gwyne droo the churchyard to work, when all at once he sees the stoan top o' one 'o the tombs begin to move. He stopped short, and stared wi' all the eyes he'd got, when up goos the stoan higher, and a man's face peeps out of one corner, and zays: 'I zay, mayet, can ye tell me what time 'tes? I've heerd my father zay he's hear lifted hes hat clane off hes head; a couldn't move but stood there staren like a stuck pig; but when Mussel axed 'en what time 'twas, he roared out, and run back prid near frightened to death. He run into the vust house a come to, and zays to the people ; 'Whatever wull become on us! the dead vokes in the churchyard be gitten out o' their graaves,' He was reglar terrified, and it gid 'en sich a turn he couldn't goo to work that day. Zometimes aaterwards he vound out the rights on't, and he and Mussell and t'others had many a laugh about it.'

Aston A. Long, Dialect of the Isle of Wight with Tales and Anecdotes, *(1931)*

12 · HOMES AND GARDENS

Two Freshwater Cottages

Tennyson and a companion while out on a walk were discussing picturesque cottages which artists delighted in painting, all thatched roofs and concealing ivy, which hid the real life within.

There was one such cottage that we used to pass in our walks that was inhabited by a family living a half-nomadic life, the aged father habitually clad in a blanket that he wore like a mantle with the air of a noble savage. The parlour could never be entered because its ceiling hung down as a bag, pressing against the door. One of the bedrooms above was turned into a sty, where two pigs passed a very dirty existence, without the ventilation that was afforded to a still more picturesque cottage with which we were acquainted, by the absence of much of the thatch and all the ceiling from its bedroom. Through its open rafters the wind and rain found free entrance, to the complete unconcern of the owner, who had built the shanty years before and ever after left it severely alone.

Agnes Grace Weld, Glimpses of Tennyson, *(1903)*

Niton Cottages in 1800

The villagers in Niton were distinctly advantaged by being part of the smuggling trade. In the early 1830s they, exceptionally, owned their own homes and this summary made at the turn of the eighteenth century shows a community of reasonably comfortable cottagers, still with language links with France.

Each cottage has a garden and some an orchard, the apples being made into cider for home consumption. Potatoes and other vegetables are grown, enabling the cottager to keep a pig. The pork of this pig and bread, and sometimes only bread is their food. Milk or beer they never taste at home. Their usual drink is coarse low-price tea, often without sugar and always without milk.

The women do little outdoor labour beyond a little weeding or stone-picking. Even within doors the use of the wheel or the knitting needles is totally unknown. This leisure . . . has one good effect, it makes the mothers better and more wholesome nurses, and induces them to keep themselves and children clean and tight, and contributes . . . to the healthy and good looks universally met with . . . There are few instances of extreme pinching poverty to be met with . . . They still retain several corrupted French words.

Hampshire Repository *vol. 2, (1801)*

Modern Country Cottages

In 1936 three cottages were built in St. Laurence, designed by M.H. Baillie Scott, a successful Arts and Crafts architect who developed the cottage into a modern home for middle class families. Baillie Scott set out his views on the then housing scene by describing his new houses and what he had intended in their building.

In order to develop the English countryside on lines so admirably initiated by our forefathers, it would seem reasonable to study closely the work of the past that remains to us.

A cottage is still a shelter from the elements, where we may be cool in summer and warm in winter and its rooms still require only the three essential features of door, windows and fireplace.

The fireplaces are brick and these are the same as the brick of the house, conveying the impression of being part of the house itself. They are quite simple in design and will not irritate us by all those fussy arrangements of tiles and brick which are too prevalent nowadays.

The windows are wooden casements opening outwards and in their fittings, as well as the doors, we recognise nothing that has been made by the gross, sold out of a shop, or chosen from a catalogue.

Concessions to modern requirements are to be found in the bathroom with its constant supply of hot and cold water, and even in the fixed basins in the bedrooms!

The appointments of the table are kept in a roomy cupboard which opens both from the dining room and pantry, and this closely adjoins the sink.

In describing such a modest home as this Ruskin has said, 'More than this few can need,' and such a dictum is more true today than it ever was, and until we acquire a new scale of values, and domestic service rises to its proper place in the scene, there will still remain the 'servant problem', to distract our housewives and make larger houses a burden too much to be borne. In such a roomy cottage they may find a release from worry and rest for their souls.

M.H. Baillie Scott, Country Building in England, (*1936*)

An Extraordinary House

Mr. and Mrs. Frederick Attrill lived in an ordinary house in Cambridge Road, East Cowes, which Frederick made so extraordinary that it became a tourist attraction.

Their house is a unique attraction to visitors. Since advancing years caused him to give up his employment Mr. Attrill's hobby has been the decoration of the outside of his house with sea-shells, and it is a wonderful sight. Various ornaments have also been used in this extraordinary decoration, which covers both sides of the side entrance, reaching as far as the prettily laid out garden, a distance of over 200ft., and half of the front of the house is similarly decorated. The entire work, which has taken years to complete, has been done by Mr. Attrill himself, who has shown wonderful patience as well as artistry. Thousands of

shells have been used, a very large quantity of them having been collected at Woodside, Wootton. There are a few large and rare shells from distant lands which foreign visitors who have inspected the house have sent to Mr. Attrill. The veteran is naturally very proud of his work, on which he has been complimented by many visitors. An influential American gentleman, Mr. Howard Mannington, who inspected the Shell House last year, stated that he had seen nothing like it in his travels . . .
Isle of Wight County Press, May 9, (1925)

Sir John Oglander's Garden at Brading

John Oglander returned to his family home East Nunwell in 1607 after his marriage to Frances More of Loseley, near Guildford. The old house was very decayed and the first task of the young couple was to rebuild it, adding a new wing which gave them a parlour and a book room. But John Oglander was also an enthusiastic gardener, spending time and money in creating beautiful gardens and orchards at Nunwell.

. . . his *Commonplace Book* contains quite detailed references to the garden at Nunwell. The earliest reference occurs in 1625 when he states:
'I built the house on East Nunwell, together with the brewhouse, barn, stable, Warren, gardens, orchards, Hoppegardens, bowling green, and all other things thereunto adjacent.'
In about 1632 a more detailed description of the garden is given:
'I have with my own hands planted two young orchards at Nunwell: the lower with pippins, pearmains, putles, hornies and other good apples and all sorts of good pears: in the other, cherries damsons and plums. In the upper garden, apricocks, mellecatoons [melons] and figs. In the Parlour Garden in one knot French flowers and tulips of all sorts: some roots cost me 10d a root. In the Court, vines and apricocks, in the Bowling Green the vine and an infinity of raspberries.'
. . . Sir John Oglander confesses that 'I have been so foolish as to bestow more money than a wise man would have done in flowers for the garden.' It is likely that Sir John Oglander was the first really dedicated amateur gardener on the Isle of Wight and it was his proud boast of the Nunwell grounds that 'Of a rude chase, I have now made it a fit place for any gentleman.'
Vicky Basford, Historic Parks and Gardens of the Isle of Wight, (1989)

Whippingham Rectory in the mid-nineteenth Century

Rowland Prothero, the son of the rector, later became a member of Parliament and Minister of Agriculture. In the 1930s he remembered his rectory childhood as being part of another world.

In the Isle of Wight three-quarters of a century ago necessity threw every household on its own resources for social entertainment or actual food. Life in the widest sense was home-made. The seclusion of each household was increased by its economic isolation. Once a day came the postman. Once a week the butcher called for orders. No other tradesman, so far as I remember came regularly to the rectory. Fish was fetched from West Cowes. Groceries were sent from London. Milk and butter, eggs and poultry, fruit and vegetables were supplied from home resources. The weekly bakings were an event. When fresh the bread was delicious and its crust unforgettably sweet and crisp. There was, however, one drawback. The batch had to be consumed, if not in the dining room, at least in the nursery and the 'servants' hall. By the fifth day the bread was so dry and the crust so tough that it was time to test the philosophy of the river and to remember that only when the ebb was at its lowest did the tide begin to flow. We brewed our own beer. I cannot remember the time when I did not have my little silver mug filled with beer at my dinner. We even made our own soap and pomatum, perfumed, after old-fashioned recipes, with a variety of scents. Wax candles were used downstairs; but in the nurseries we only had tallow candles. Snuffer trays and snuffers, now preserved as curiosities, were necessities of daily life.

After the [Sunday] morning service, my father came into the servants' hall and carved a sirloin of beef into dinners for the half-dozen or more old people who could not come to church. They were represented by a daughter or grandchild or a neighbour, who brought with them their basin or dish tied up in a handkerchief. It was my duty to add the baked potato.'

Lord Ernle (Rowland Prothero), Whippingham to Westminster, (1938)

22 Orchard Street, Newport

Number 22 occupied a central position . . . Fourteen feet of frontage, a door opening out on to the pavement and a passage leading straight through to the scullery . . . built onto the rear of the main building.

The first door off the passage gave access to the front room, the holy of holies, from which I was totally excluded, except at Christmas, when the fire in the open grate and the alien surroundings were as exciting as the presents themselves. Should a visitor call and be shown into the front room it was someone of importance A staircase leading to the two bedrooms separated the front and rear rooms and a tongued and grooved door fastened with a large wooden button, shut the staircase off from the passage.

The rear or living room is indelibly stamped on my mind; open the door outwards into the passage with the enquiring call of 'Mum' and all was well with the world. She was always there. The kitchener seemed to occupy almost the whole of the far wall. It was black, gleaming and always glowing, an oven on one side, a highly polished tap on the other and an assortment of pots and pans on the top, always bubbling and hissing. A round table occupied the centre of the room, prominently displaying an oil lamp. When day was done, the curtains drawn, we sat around the table in the light and warmth of that lamp, reading papers, books and comics, and there was an inner feeling of content that no money could buy.

Bill Shepard, Newport Isle of Wight Remembered, (*1984*)

The Garden at Owl Cottage, Mottistone.

When Hannah and Leslie Hutchinson bought Owl Cottage it was a simple farm labourer's cottage in a field. The cottage was carefully modernized and work began to make a garden out of the field. The result was a perfect cottage garden which thousands of visitors have enjoyed over the years.

Visiting Owl Cottage in the Isle of Wight in summer is rather like stepping into the pages of Beatrix Potter. Created and gardened by two sisters, Mrs. Hutchinson and Miss Leaning, it is the cottage of everyone's childhood memories. A rich and wonderful profusion of delphiniums, poppies, phlox, campanulas greets you as you come in through the garden gate, itself festooned with roses. The picture is framed by the thatched roof and thick walls of the ancient clunch-built cottage and the leaves and branches of an ornamental cherry, 'Pink Perfection', which offers its contribution in spring. Once the delphiniums are over, the starring role is taken up by a host of dahlias.

Scattered throughout the garden is a splendid selection of roses, often grown with clematis scrambling through and over them. In one of the few attempts at formality, a line of 'Frencham' roses with their deep scarlet velvety flowers lines the path to the part of the garden behind the house. The delicious scent of the old-fashioned rose 'Madame Pierre Oger' fills this area in summer, but it really needs continuous dead-heading, says Mrs. Hutchinson. Around the lawn to the side of the house, dominated by a massive weeping cherry, are the roses 'Fritz Nobis', 'Queen of Denmark' and 'Chaucer' with its pink candy-sugar blooms, an offspring of 'Constance Spry' . . . Yet more clematis flourish here, usually entwined with roses or other shrubs . . .

The border close to the outbuildings is devoted to more unusual plants, including a bed of *Alstroemeria* Ligtu hybrids, all in soft art shades, which make a wonderful show in midsummer.

The sisters generally aim to keep the garden a typical cottage garden, with a continuous succession of flowers. The season starts with over twenty Japanese flowering cherry trees, which, along with the bulbs, provide a glorious spring display before the rose and clematis come into their own in summer.

Judy Johnson and Susan Berry, English Private Gardens, (*1991*)

Behind the Scenes at Westover, Calbourne

Westover is the elegant country house built by John Nash on the edge of Calbourne village, looking down on the cottages and church. Mona, the daughter of the coachman, was employed as cook when she was eighteen in 1932. She experienced the last years of the old way of living in a manor house before the Second World War extinguished it for ever.

Each day at 10am the mistress came to the kitchen to give cook her orders, and everything had to be spick and span by then . . . The 'fitted kitchen' comprised three wooden benches joined together, and a scrubbed wooden dresser which held the copper utensils. All cooking was done on the kitchen range. This had two large ovens which had to be blackleaded, while in front was a large white hearth which had to be whitened every morning. This was surrounded by a steel fender, cleaned by buffing it with emery paper . . .

The large wooden table was kept clear at one end, while a cloth covered the other half so that the staff's meals could be served there. In times of plenty, staff had their own menu, but after the death duties had been paid, staff ate the remainder from the family meals. Breakfast was served at 8.30am in silver entree dishes, with choices such as scrambled egg, kidneys, and fish dishes. After May (parlour maid) had washed up the breakfast dishes, all the lamps had to be filled with paraffin. This was for the kitchen, the staff room, pantry, dining room, two drawing rooms, library, hallway, front hall and scullery.

Lunch would comprise meat and vegetables, a pudding and Stilton cheese and port. Tea was served at four o'clock and consisted of small sandwiches plus cakes served on a cake stand. Dinner would be soup, with a meat or fish dish, a sweet, then a savoury.

In summer there were tennis parties. May made the claret cup, and Mona made ice cream in the hand churn from real cream and strawberries (enough for twenty!) Ice for the ice cream came via the fishman and it was used with saltpetre to pack round the mixture.

Winter shooting parties had hotpots served in earthenware pots, or alternatively, meat pies. Then there were apple cobs (like apple dumpling in short crust pastry) with whiskey liqueur, which Mona made from whitecurrants. This was rounded off with bread and cheese and beer. About a dozen guns would attend, and some three or four would stay in the house as guests.

'Aunt Liz' was the laundry maid. She had a room with a huge copper, tubs for rinsing and a wringer. There was a stove, with a ledge all round to hold the clothes. This stove used coke. The ironing room was bigger than the washing room, with large drying racks. Ten irons, each weighing 14 lbs, were in use and a mangle was used to flatten the sheets and towels. All evening shirts were starched to keep them stiff. That poor lady also had to push a wheelbarrow up the drive over rough ground, with all the wet clothes to be hung out on lines.

The Isle of Wight Federation of Women's Institutes, Isle of Wight Within Living Memory, (1994)

A Poet's Garden at Orchard's Bay

Ours is an old garden, with lawns all the smoother for the rugged setting of the landscape. Even the tall myrtles – one of them fifteen feet high – have been rounded by age till their massive dark green heads have the smoothness of sea-worn boulders. They must have been crowded with their little rosy buds, and lighted by their delicate stars of white blossom for a hundred autumns or more.

The long house of worn grey stone, with twisted red Elizabethan chimneys, is old, too, in its main structure; and, although it has been enlarged by more than one generation the workmanship was so good that it is difficult to say where or when the extensions were made. Engravings in old books of a hundred and fifty years back show the house as it stands today; and the central part, like the gardener's deep-thatched cottage at the outer gate, has weathered three centuries of island sun.

Most of the windows look south, and when the moon hangs over the sea, and the moon-path lies trembling on the water, in a direct line with them, they are all 'magic casements'. One, especially; for it looks to the sea over a pool fed by a perennial spring; and a falling brook, with tall clusters of arum lilies growing at the water's edge along their rocky banks. They have been growing there for years, with their roots under water; and their young leaves are green throughout the winter. There were hundreds of these lilies in the spring of last year, lifting their great white chalices against the clumps of purple aubrieta that clothe the stony slope behind them, and give warmth to what otherwise might be too cold a loveliness. Above the pool, not six yards from the window, there stands a thirty-foot dragon's blood palm tree. It might well have been nourished on the blood of that very dragon that guarded the golden apples of the Hesperides garden – the dragon from which it may derive its name. But the glimmer of crimson on the low grey wall of the terrace below it is nothing more sinister than some rambling roses which are in bloom during the greater part of the year. The palm tree also has its flowering time, and every year juts out great bunches of little white blossoms which, seen from below, look like lilies of the valley.

Alfred Noyes, Orchard's Bay, *(1939)*

13 · CARISBROOKE CASTLE

The castle is the centre of the Island physically and historically. It was the home of royal representatives from the middle ages to the twentieth century. William the Conqueror made a dramatic visit early in his reign to arrest Bishop Odo in the great hall; our present Queen visited on a grand state occasion when Lord Louis Mountbatten was appointed Governor of the Isle of Wight. Millions of visitors have passed through the medieval gates into the courtyard, for the castle has been accessible since the eighteenth century.

The Royal Prisoner

The Civil War in the seventeenth century shot Carisbrooke into the national political scene when Charles I was imprisoned there for a year before his trial and execution in January 1649. Then the castle was rapidly transformed into a suitable residence for the king, paintings were brought from Hampton Court, and an inventory made in 1650 gives some idea of the rich and colourful surroundings in which he lived.

It must not, however, be supposed that the fittings of [his] apartments were merely limited to the rude military appointments of the day, for by a reference to the appraisement of the furniture and plate within the castle after the king's execution, it is evident that regal splendour prevailed therein, for the appraisement is so minute in its descriptive detail, that a most vivid idea may readily be conceived . . .

> An inventory of goods in Carisbrooke Castle, appraised the 17th October, 1650
> One standing bedstead, covered with crimson velvet, trimmed with gold and silver lace, and fringed, with all the furniture thereunto belonging £120.0.0
> One crimson damask window curtain, of seven breadths, lined with perpetuana £7.0.0
> Two small window curtains, of crimson damask, lined as aforesaid £3.10.0
> One watchet velvet necessary stool £1.10.0
> One foot carpet £4.10.0
> Two small Turkey carpets £12.0.0
> Eight pieces of Arras hangings £210.0.0
> Eight pieces of Turkey hangings of the Roman Emperors £90.0.0
> Two pieces of tapestry imagery £12.0.0
> Twelve folding stooles of green velvet framed with gold and silver fringe £8.0.0
> Two green velvet chairs, two cushions and a foot-stool £7.0.0
> One standing bedstead, covered with green velvet, laced and fringed with gold and silver, with all the furniture thereunto belonging suitable £130.0.0
> One small chair of crimson velvet, which was Queen Elizabeth's £0.10.0

George Hillier, A Narrative of the Attempted Escapes of Charles the First from Carisbrooke Castle, *(1852)*

The King Plans to Escape

Charles I began to look for ways to escape almost as soon as he arrived in Carisbrooke. Careful planning was needed and the young man who took charge of this was already in place as groom of the bedchamber. Henry Firebrace made careful arrangements within and without the castle and all was prepared for an attempt in March 1648.

The plan for the King's escape was founded on the fact that the inner court of the castle did not seem to be patrolled at night, so there was little chance of interference while the king was climbing out of his window. He was to lower himself down to the courtyard with a rope previously provided by Firebrace, and the two of them would then cross the courtyard and go up to the battlements on the curtain wall, presumably on the south side which was remote from the officers' quarters against the north curtain and the gatehouse and guard rooms on the west. Here Firebrace was to pay out a longer rope with a stick fastened across the end for the King to sit on, so that he could be lowered down to the top of the bank at the base of the curtain wall – a drop of fifteen feet. Negotiating on his own the scramble down the bank into the sunken 'covered way', the King would find as his last obstacle the Elizabethan fortifications beyond the curtain wall. The drop here was only nine feet, and he would be helped down by Osborne and Worsley, who would be waiting there with a spare horse ready saddled, and pistols and riding boots for the King when he came over the wall. Waiting on the coast 'in a convenient place' was John Newland, with 'a lusty Boat' ready to take the King to whichever port he chose. The scheme was worked out in detail and every stage of it carefully checked.

All the arrangements were now complete, and the night of Monday, March 20 was settled for the attempt. Unobtrusively the escape boat came on station, and as darkness closed over the castle Osborne and Worsley cautiously approached the outer wall with their three horses. One by one the candles went out in various apartments of the castle, and Firebrace came into the courtyard, his ears straining for any unexpected movements of the night sentries. The convivial sounds coming from the guard rooms in the gatehouse had alcoholic overtones that Firebrace found reassuring. As his eyes became accustomed to the starlight he looked up at the two small windows of the King's bedroom, thirteen feet above the courtyard. The light there, like all the others, had now gone out, but he knew the prisoner was there at the window, ears alert for a signal from outside. The rope for the first stage of the escape had been safely smuggled into the room. The elaborate plan was about to begin.

With a final look round to make sure the courtyard was empty, Firebrace approached the King's window and sent a small stone tinkling up against the glass. He held his breath as he heard the window being furtively opened, followed by a scuffling noise as the King began to squeeze out. Occasional gasps indicated the effort that was being expended then Firebrace heard the king groaning, and at this point all his optimism drained away. He knew too well what had happened.

Firebrace and the king had already had some argument about the width of the opening in the barred window, Firebrace maintaining that it would be necessary to remove the bar. The King replied that he had tried, one night, fitting his head through, and he considered the opening was wide enough. Firebrace, still unconvinced, proposed widening the opening a little 'by cutting the plate the Casement shut to at the bottome: w[hi]ch then might have been easily put by'. He probably meant by this, cutting through the seat of the base of the bar and bending it aside. The King replied, with some justification, that previous tampering of this sort would mean running the risk of discovery. He told Firebrace to go on with all the other arrangements, leaving him to worry about the window, which he was sure he could negotiate.

This miscalculation proved fatal to the carefully laid escape, and it was no satisfaction to Firebrace, fretting impotently down in the courtyard, to be thus proved right. By now, if he was interpreting correctly the sounds from above, the King was tightly wedged in the window, unable to move in either direction. Firebrace peered up anxiously in an effort to pierce the darkness, his mind racing with possible ways of meeting the crisis. Then he saw something that at least partly reassured him. A candle had been lit in the window, a signal that the King had got back inside and abandoned the escape. The mortifying sound of distant laughter from the guard rooms served only to emphasize how nearly the King had come to taking his jailors by surprise.

Firebrace morosely made his way to the appointed place on the castle wall. Somewhere in the darkness beyond it, his two fellow-conspirators were keeping their bleak and hazardous rendezvous. He had to get them away before some chance patrol stumbled across them. To hail them at forty yards distance from the curtain wall would probably have penetrated even the fuddled hearing of the guards; but he still had his handful of stones and he proceeded to throw these, one by one, at the spot where his friends were waiting. Presently he knew from the subdued jingle of harness that they were moving away. The plan had collapsed in ruins, but he had at least performed his last duty for the night: he had brushed over the trail. Now at last he could go to bed.'

Jack D. Jones, The Royal Prisoner, (1965)

A Treasure in Carisbrooke Castle

John Meade Falkner's smuggling adventure story, Moonfleet, published in 1898, is still a good read today, especially for Islanders, as the dramatic highlight of the story takes place in Carisbrooke Castle. Falkner takes some liberties with history, making Colonel Mohune of Moonfleet, Dorset, one of Charles I's guards. The king bribes him with a large diamond taken from his crown to allow him to escape, but the treacherous Mohune betrays him as the king remains stuck in his bedroom window. The diamond is lost for about one hundred years until

John Trenchard, a fifteen year old boy from Moonfleet village, deciphers a coded message which leads him to the castle. There he and his companion Elzevir Block meet the castle jailor and together they enter the well-house.

The building was open to the roof and the first thing to be seen in it was that tread-wheel of which Elzevir had spoken. It was a great open wheel of wood, ten or twelve feet across, and very like a mill wheel, only the space between the rims was boarded flat, but had treads nailed on it to give foothold to a donkey. The patient beast was lying loose stabled on some straw in the corner of the room. At the side of the wheel was the well-mouth, a dark, round opening with a low parapet round it, rising two feet from the floor . . .

[Elzevir] had taken the coil of twine from his arm and was undoing it. 'We will let an end of this down the well,' he said, 'and I have made a knot in it at eighty feet. This lad thinks the treasure is in the well wall, eighty feet below us, so when the knot is on well lip we shall know we have the right depth.' . . .

'I will get into the bucket,' Elzevir said, turning to me, 'and this good man will lower me gently by the break until I reach the string-end down below. Then I will shout, and so fix you the wheel and give me time to search.' . . .

'No, master, that cannot be; 'tis my place to go, being smaller and a lighter weight than thou; and thou shalt stop here and help this gentleman to lower me down . . . Art sure the well is clean, and that no deadly gases lurk below?'

'Thou mayest be sure I knew the well was sweet before I let thee talk of going down,' he answered. 'For yesterday we lowered a candle to the water, and the flame burned bright and steady; and where the candle lives, there man lives too. But thou art right: these gases change from day to day, and we will try the thing again. so bring the candle, Master Jailer.'

The jailer brought a candle fixed on a wooden triangle, which he was wont to show strangers who came to see the well, and lowered it on a string . . . I watched the candle sink into that cavernous depth, and from a bright flame turn into a little twinkling star, and then to a mere point of light. At last it rested on the water, and there was a shimmer where the wood frame had set ripples moving . . .

They pulled the candle up forthwith and put it in my hand, and I flung the plasterer's hammer into the bucket, where it hung above the well, and then got in myself. The turnkey stood at the break-wheel, and Elzevir leant over the parapet to steady the rope. 'Art sure thou canst do it, lad?' he said, speaking low, and putting his hand kindly on my shoulder. 'Are head and heart sure? Thou art my diamond, and I would rather lose all other diamonds in the world than aught should come to thee. So, if thou doubtest let me go, or let not any go at all.'

'Never doubt, master,' I said, touched by tenderness, and wrung his hand. 'My head is sure;' . . .

The bucket was large, for all the turnkey had tried to frighten me into think it small, and I could crouch in it low enough to feel safe of not falling out. They lowered me gently enough, so that I was able to take stock of the way the wall was made, and found that for the most part it was cut through solid chalk; but here and there where the chalk failed or was broken away, they had lined the walls with brick, patching them now on this side, now on that, and now all round. By degrees the light, which was dim even overground that rainy day, died out in the well, till all was black as night but for my candle, and far overhead I could see the well-mouth, white and round like a lustreless full-moon.

I kept an eye on Elzevir's cord that hung down the well-side, and when I saw it was coming to a finish, shouted to them to stop, and they brought the bucket up near level with the end of it, so I knew I was about eighty feet deep. Then I raised myself, standing up in the bucket and holding by the rope, and began to look round, knowing not all the while what I looked for, but thinking to see a hole in the wall, or perhaps the diamond itself shining out of a cranny. But I could perceive nothing; and what made it more difficult was, that the walls here were lined completely with small flat bricks, and looked much the same all round. I examined these bricks as closely as I might . . . but to little purpose. They could see my candle moving round and round from the well-top, and knew no doubt what I was at, but Master Turnkey grew impatient, and shouted down, 'What are you doing? have you found nothing? can you see no treasure?' 'No,' I called back, 'I can see nothing,' and then, 'are you sure, Master Block, that you measured the plummet true to eighty feet?'

I heard them talking together, but could not make out what they said, for the bim-bom and echo of the well, till Elzevir shouted again, 'They say this floor has been raised; you must try lower.'

Then the bucket began to move lower, slowly, and I crouched down in it again, not wishing to look too much into the unfathomable, dark abyss below . . . when the bucket stopped some six feet lower down, I fell again to diligently examining the walls. They were still built of shallow bricks, and scanning them course by course as before, I could see at first nothing, but as I moved my eyes downwards they were brought up by a mark scratched on a brick close to the hanging plummet-line . . .

Though it was very slight, so that I think not one in a thousand would ever have noticed it at all, yet it stopped my eyes and brought up my thoughts suddenly, because I knew by instinct that it had something to do with me and what I sought.

The sides of this well are dry and clean . . . so these bricks were also dry and clean, and this mark as sharp as if made yesterday, though the issue showed that 'twas put there a very long time ago. Now the mark was not deeply or regularly graven, but roughly scratched, as I have known boys score their names, or alphabet letters, or dates, on the alabaster figures that lie in Moonfleet Church. And here, too, was scored a letter of the alphabet a plain Y, and would have passed for nothing more perhaps to any not born in Moonfleet; but to me it was the *cross pall*, or black Y of the Mohunes, under whose shadow we were all brought up. So as soon as I saw that, I knew I was near what I sought . . .

I shouted up the well that they must bring me nearer in to the side. They understood what I would be at, and slipped a noose over the well-rope and so drew it in to the side, and made it fast till I should give the word to loose again. Thus I was brought close to the well-wall, and the marked brick near the level of my face when I stood up in the bucket. There was nothing to show that this brick had been tampered with, nor did it sound hollow when tapped, though when I came to look closely at the joints, it seemed as though there was more cement than usual about the edges. But I never doubted what we sought was to be found behind it, and so got to work at once, fixing the wooden frame of the candle in the fastening of the chain, and chipping out the mortar setting with the plasterer's hammer . . .

Soon I had the mortar out of the joints, and the brick loose enough to prise it forward, by putting the edge of the hammer in the crack. I lifted it clean out and put it in the bucket, to see later on, in case of need, if there was a hollow for anything to be hidden in; but never had occasion to look at it again, for there, behind the brick, was a little hole in the wall, and in the hole what I sought. I had my fingers in the hole too quick for words, and brought out a little parchment bag, and this little bag had something of the size of a small pebble that rattled in the inside of it. Only I knew that this was no pebble, and set to work to get it out. But though the little bag was parched and dry, 'twas not so easily torn and at last I struck off the corner of it with the sharp edge of my hammer against the bucket. Then I shook it carefully, and out into my hand there dropped a pure crystal as big as a walnut. I had never in my life seen a diamond, either large or small - yet if I had not known that Blackbeard had buried a diamond, and if we had not come hither of set purpose to find it, I should not have doubted that what I had in my hand was a diamond, and this of matchless size and brilliance. It was cut into many facets, and though there was little or no light in the well save my candle, there seemed to be in this stone the light of a thousand fires that flashed out, sparkling red, blue and green, as turned it between my fingers. I was, as it were, dazzled by its brilliance, and by the possibilities of wealth it contained, and had, perhaps, a desire to keep it to myself as long as might be; so that I thought nothing of the two who were waiting for me at the well-mouth, till I was suddenly called back by the harsh voice of the turnkey, crying as before -

'What are you doing? have you found nothing?'

'Yes,' I shouted back, 'I have found the treasure; you can pull me up.'

J. Meade Falkner, Moonfleet, (1898)

The Island's War Memorial

Although the Isle of Wight was part of the county of Hampshire there was a natural wish to have a memorial in the Island for those local men who had died in the 1914-18 war, and efforts to achieve this began in 1918. But it proved to be a very protracted undertaking and it was only in 1929 that the memorial was completed. There were difficulties from the beginning when it was decided that Saint Nicholas-in-Castro was to be the site. A few years previously the ruined eighteenth century chapel built on the foundations of the medieval chapel had been rebuilt as a memorial to Charles I and there was some opposition to sharing it as a war memorial.

Happily, an initial decision to inscribe on stone panels in the chapel the names of all those who died on active service was never abandoned. It was a remarkable undertaking, and proved costly, but the result was

a richly decorated collegiate-style interior, and on the walls are the stone
panels with two thousand names, still as sharp as when they were first
cut.

The County Press *followed its progress from beginning to end.*

4 May 1918 From John Fardell, Morton Manor, Brading
. . . Sir Charles Seely stated that he was certain the Isle of Wight would
certainly wish to have a memorial in the Island. I venture to point out
that there is only one suitable site for such a memorial and that is
Carisbrooke Castle. In the Castle is the chapel of St. Nicholas, recently
rebuilt, and still a mere casket internally, and yet to be perfected and
made beautiful to the honour and glory of God.

2 February 1919. The Isle of Wight memorial should consist of a
record of the names of all the Island men who have fallen in the war on
the walls of the ante-chapel of St. Nicholas in Carisbrooke Castle.

21 June 1919. From Douglas Macleane, Canon of Salisbury,
Branksome Park: 'As a member of the original committee for re-building
and re-dedication of the little fallen sanctuary of St. Nicholas-within-
Carisbrooke Castle, in religious memory of King Charles the Martyr,
may I be allowed to assure you of the deep distress with which members
of the committee have heard of the proposed alienation of the chapel to
the purposes of a war memorial church. I suppose we have no redress for
this wrong, but can only protest. A revolutionary spirit is abroad, and all
rights are in the melting pot . . .

27 July 1919. Mr. Percy Stone, F.S.A. reported that the plans of the
memorial in the chapel at Carisbrooke Castle had been approved by
H.M. Office of Works. He had visited the works of Messrs. Garrett and
Haysom at Southampton . . . next month they would start work at the
chapel in connection with the first part of the scheme, which included all
the stone work in the chapel itself, panel carving, and cutting the names
of over 1600 fallen thereon.

30 July 1925. On Sunday afternoon H.R.H. Princess Beatrice was
present at the re-opening service of the chapel of St. Nicholas. The first
portion of the memorial work which has been completed consists of
panelling with wood and the painting of the interior of the roof,
provision of a vestry with other improvements at the west end, and
preparation of the walls to receive the Hoptonwood stone which has
been designed to receive the names of the fallen.

3 October 1925. On the occasion of her visit to the Island, during

Cowes Week, Her Majesty the Queen inspected the Island war memorial in the Chapel of St. Nicholas, at Carisbrooke Castle, and expressed regret that it was still incomplete, only the names of men belonging to the I.W. Rifles, who lost their lives in the war being as yet included. Her Majesty also very graciously expressed a wish to assist in furthering the work of completion. It is proposed to organise a fête at Carisbrooke Castle, to be held during the next Cowes Week, at which Her Majesty has signified her intention of being present.

14 September 1929. The County War Memorial

Restored as a building in 1904 to the memory of King Charles the First, the Chapel of St. Nicholas-within-the-Castle of Carisbrooke has been completed as the all-Island War Memorial, which is to be dedicated on the apposite feast of St. Michael and All Angels (Sunday September 29th.) On the side walls between the windows and in the ante chapel, on panels of polished Hoptonwood stone are cut the names – some 2000 in number – of those who made the supreme sacrifice.

A Present for a Princess

Princess Beatrice celebrated her 80th birthday on April 14th 1937, but she had to wait until the autumn for a special birthday gift from the people of the Isle of Wight. Her present was one she had long wished for, the 'ancient organ' which was then believed to have been played by Princess Elizabeth, daughter of Charles I, during the short time she lived at Carisbrooke Castle.

On Sunday afternoon the Island people delighted to honour their esteemed Royal Governor, H.R.H. Princess Beatrice. In the presence of a large gathering in the ancient courtyard of her residence, Carisbrooke Castle, Her Royal Highness was the obviously delighted recipient of a novel and interesting gift from her Island friends as an 80th birthday present and as a mark of the profound appreciation of her outstandingly devoted and valuable services to the community as Royal Governor for the long period of 41 years.

It was known that Her Royal Highness had always been interested in an ancient organ belonging to Lady Maud Warrender, which, according to a strong local tradition was used by Princess Elizabeth during her period of captivity at Carisbrooke Castle. It was known, too, that her

Royal Highness coveted the instrument to restore it to the castle and those who were considering some public presentation ascertained that the organ could be purchased for the purpose at £400. Consequently a subscription list was opened to raise this sum in small donations from the people of the Island, and this was soon accomplished.

The presentation followed the last of the customary services in the chapel of St. Nicholas in the Castle, which are held during the Royal Governor's stay each summer.

Lady Mottistone then made the presentation in the following terms; 'Your Royal Highness – May we ask you to accept this romantic birthday gift, subscribed to by so many of your Isle of Wight friends, as an expression of the respect, loyalty, and affection you have inspired in us. We pray that for years to come you may be enabled to enjoy its beauty..'

Acknowledging the gift, Princess Beatrice said; 'I am most touched and deeply grateful to all my kind friends, acquaintances and others in the Isle of Wight and elsewhere who have wished to combine in presenting me with such a beautiful gift to commemorate my 80th birthday and the many years of my governorship. Nothing could give me more pleasure or be more valued by me than this small organ, having belonged to the unfortunate young Princess Elizabeth and having been played on by her during her captivity within these walls. It is my hope that this most valuable and historic gift may find a permanent home in this castle. Once more I thank you all very much.'

A sonnet written by Alfred Noyes was read by the poet as part of the presentation. The opening lines are a picture of the Island in winter.

This little isle, this garden of the seas
    Where primrose clusters wake on Christmas morn,
    And, while the last rose lingers on the thorn,
The first wild violet sweetens the salt breeze;
Chalk downs, and broken cliffs, and sun swept leas
    Where black-nosed lambs and crocuses are born;
    and those white Needles, by the Atlantic worn,
What ships they have known, and what great memories!
This island, madam, keeps its memories green;
    And there's one memory, to yourself most dear,
    More precious far than sceptre, crown, or throne,

One name, far lovelier than the name of queen;
  Whose great true heart still draws her daughter near,
And makes this island – and our love – you own.
Isle of Wight County Press, *Saturday October 9, (1937)*

The Chamber Organ

The chamber organ displayed at Carisbrooke Castle Museum has generally been regarded as Flemish in origin, having been built by E. Hoffheimer in 1602. Its first owner was apparently John Graham, Earl of Montrose, whose coat of arms is carved at the top of the instrument. Princess Beatrice bequeathed the organ to the Minister of Works to be maintained in Carisbrooke Castle, and it passed into his care on her death in 1944. It is the oldest playing organ in Britain still in playing order and is one of the few instruments in this country still kept on the meantone scale.
Carisbrooke Castle Museum

The French raids on the Isle of Wight in the fourteenth century left a long memory of fire and pillage. Sir John Oglander recorded the siege of Carisbrooke Castle in his notes written in the early part of the seventeenth century, describing the death of the French commander. He named the particular type of bow used as a tiller bow. This was later wrongly transcribed as a silver bow and it is this description Percy Stone used in his twentieth century poem of the historic event.

This is the Rime of the Silver Bow and the Lord of Stenbury,
Whose name and fame will live for aye in Island history.
Then health to the bow and the archer bold and the bolt of
    the ashen-tree, –
The bow that laid the archer low and set our Island free.

With sword and spear and banner
They've marshalled on the strand:
War's flames lights up the heavens,
    red ruin rules the land,
Three towns laid stark in ashes

Betoken the advance
Of pitiless invaders
Grim soldiery of France.
They've swung the Newport provosts
Above their Meeting Hall,
And sworn to seize the Castle
And raze its circling wall.

Quoth bold Sir Hugh our Captain,
A doughty knight and true,
'Our walls shall go to ruin,
Ere ever they win through.
Go, bid them raise the drawbridge:
Go bid them man the walls.
No man must hold him backward
When England's honour calls.

De Heyno, Lord of Stenbury
A wondrous bow had he,
All wrought and laid with silver
In patterns cunningly.
He stood a famous marksman
Among the archer men;
Could dent a silver penny
At three score yards and ten.
Due noted he their leader,
At morn and evening bell,
Draw near to mark the curtain
– And marked the distant well.
'A shaft should reach yon Frenchman,
If well and truly laid:
Stout patron saint of archers,
Good Hubert, be my aid.'

From belt he plucked a quarrel,
And fitted it to bow.
'An give me leave, Sir Captain,

I'll lay that braggart low.'
'Ay, certes,' answered Tyrrell,
    'A fair and famous deed,
For, could we smite their leader,
    'Twould help us in our need.
I'd bid thee shoot, Sir Archer
    – All's fair in Love and War –
But, by the hail of Crecy,
    The range is over far.'
For answer swung the bow-string
    And sped the bolt amain.
St.George! The Frenchman's fallen,
    Fair stricken in the brain.

'Twas thus we held the Castle
    And checked the French advance,
And so gave time for muster
    Against the might of France.
East – West our levies gathered
    Along the Island downs,
And thrust their forces backward
    And venged our burning towns.
And while our Island story
    Drifts down the tide of time,
'Twill ever be remembered
    That's here set down in rhyme.

All honour to de Heyno
    Laud high his silver bow
That sped so true the venging bolt
    Which laid their leader low.
Percy G. Stone, Legends and Lays of the Wight, (*1912*)

14 · THE ROYAL RESIDENT

These doggerel verses retelling a true incident are typical of popular Victorian publications for working people. They were cheap to produce and sell, reflect the cottager's daily life, instil admiration for both the subject and the Queen and conclude with a worthy moral.

The Royal Umbrella

Isle of Wight is very small,
    But an enchanting spot
Rail-road and steamers whisk you there,
    As now, where will they not?

But never had the Isle till now
    Such cause for pride and boast;
The gracious Sovereign of these realms,
    Has visited its coasts.

A cottage is the poor abode,

Of Cowes's man of letters;
And yet he boasts a prouder name
     Than many of his betters.

From Whippingham to Cowes and back
     Was Scudamore's long walk;
A joyous spirit cheer'd his way
And friendly neighbours talk.

The good postmaster's wife would grieve,
     When he so late returned,
And when she saw him wet, would deem
     His pittance hardly earn'd:

One morning up the village path
     A pedlar came along:
'Buy an umbrella, 'tis my last,
     I'll sell it for a song.

'Tis gingham, but quite waterproof,
     Will neither break nor bend,
Come buy it, ma'am, and, mark my words,
     'Twill prove you husband's friend'.

She had some money in a cup
     And quickly reached it down,
The bargain's struck, the prize secured
     For less than half a-crown.

The Queen and Prince one morning strolled
     Alone by hill and plain,
When suddenly a large black cloud
     Began to sprinkle rain.

Just at that moment, round the hill
     Our postman jogged along,
Rejoicing in the bargain he
     Had got for an odd song.

He saw a lady in the rain,
     And quickly made a start;
He had the Englishman's best gift,

Politeness of the heart.

He bagg'd the letters safe, and ran
        His very best, poor fellow
In pure humanity to lend
        The lady his umbrella.

Prince Albert held the gingham o'er
        His Royal Consort's head
The postman following by command
        To Osborne House they fled

When such a heavy rain set in,
        Poor Mrs. Scudamore
Looked anxiously, and trimm'd her fire,
        As he approached the door.

'Dear heart,' she cried, 'how wet you are!
        That pedlar took me in;
He told me it was waterproof –
        You're dripping to the skin!'

'Cease your complaint, my dear,' said he
        'And, if you be loyal,
Prize that umbrella more than life,
        From this day it is Royal!'

Conclusion

    . . . A moral useful to us all
        We from this tale may glean;
By doing good to great and small
        We best shall serve out Queen.
Anon.

The Queen and Prince Albert first bought old Osborne House from
Lady Elizabeth Blachford, paying £27,814 18s 5d for it on 1 May 1845.
But they needed more land and so Barton Manor and lands owned by
Winchester College were acquired. This made the estate an economic
size, running south from the small Norris Castle property to a piece of

ground named Mount Misery. And it gave Victoria and Albert the
privacy they longed for.

Even before the settlement, Albert had sent for his proposed builder . . .
Thomas Cubitt, who had made a fortune out of developing the district
now called Belgravia. Cubitt, then in his late fifties, had been called upon
at Christmas 1844 to prepare a survey of [Old Osborne]. His report
recommended a new structure as 'less expensive in the end than the
repair of the present one.' Victoria and Albert had agreed . . . Finally on
the evening of 14 September 1846, after a lady-in-waiting threw an old
shoe into the house for luck, the royal family moved in for their first
night in the unfinished structure. Lady Lyttleton, remaining in charge of
the royal nursery, oversaw the children scampering about, each attended
by a scarlet-clad footman and Victoria called the occasion 'like a dream
to be here now in our own house, of which we laid the stone only fifteen
months ago'.

At their first dinner in Osborne House, everyone rose to drink to the
royal couple's health, and Albert responded with a housewarming hymn
of Luther's from the 128th psalm;

> So shall thy wife be in thy house
> Like vine with clusters plenteous
> Thy children sit thy table round
> Like olive plants all fresh and sound.

'The windows', Lady Lyttleton wrote, 'lighted by the brilliant lamps in
the rooms, must have been seen far out to sea.'

Stanley Weintraub, Albert Uncrowned King, (1997)

The Pavilion

This was the home of the Royal Family. It was not large compared with
country houses of its day ; the ground floor was formal, a spacious hall
from which rose the stairs, a very fine drawing room with large windows
looking out to Osborne Bay, the dining room opening from it on one
side and a billiard room on the other. On the first floor were the private
rooms; the sitting room, Prince Albert's study-dressing room and his
bathroom, the Queen's bathroom and their bedroom. On the top floor
were the children's day rooms and their night nurseries. It was much too

*small for grand gatherings and for these a marquee had to be erected on
the lawn. It was only in 1890-91 that the Durbar Wing completed the
house with its exuberant Indian Durbar room, and gave space above for
separate apartments for Princess Beatrice and her family. It was from the
outset a summer home where house and landscape were united.*

Osborne was meant from the beginning as a grand composition of
wooded hillside, clumps of nearer trees, lawns, terraces, building,
sculpture, flowers, sunlight, and the glorious views of the Solent. The
building is admirably related to its site and intelligent in plan. Above all
it was practical; it was one of the first nearly fireproof domestic
buildings intentionally so designed . . .

The brilliant colours of Victorian bedding plants were brought into
the house by large windows and by strong colours used on an ample
white ground. The paving of the open colonnades and the inner
corridors which extended them was of excellent Minton tiles on which
the arms of Great Britain and Saxony appeared in their blue, gold and
green on a ground of starch-blue scrollwork and white. The colour was
rich; the drawing-room originally had yellow satin-damask curtains and
covers, while its specially woven Aubusson carpet was made to fit round
the scagliola columns which divided the room nominally into three
sections, one end bay of the three-part room was extended by another
bay which was effectively an L around the corner, so that men could sit
or play billiards at a table designed (like its hanging lamp) by the Prince.

[The private rooms are] middle class Victorian taste bang on centre:
the many pictures hung symmetrically, the close carpeting in rather loose
patterns a bit too large, the excellent balloon-back or modified Regency
chairs, the plain woods, the chintz, the upholstery . . .

Winslow Ames, Prince Albert and Victorian Taste, (1967)

'How Happy we are Here!'

The family was never happier, never closer, than at Osborne, where
Prince Albert, in his own words, was 'partly forester, partly builder,
partly farmer and partly gardener.' 'How happy we are here!' the Queen
exclaimed.

Eleanor Stanley observed: The whole Royal family, children, Queen
and all, seem to be out the whole day long; I don't believe the Queen

thinks of reading a despatch or of doing anything in the way of business, further than scribbling her name where it is required . . . she draws a good deal, and walks and enjoys herself. The children dine and tea in the garden, and run about to their heart's content, and yesterday evening they, assisted by their august Papa, and sanctioned by the presence of their royal Mama, who was looking on washed a basketful of potatoes and shelled a ditto of peas, which they are to cook for themselves today if they are good. Did you ever hear of such happy children?

Although Osborne was a holiday home, the daily life there was spartan. The meals were simple indeed; a bit of roast meat and perhaps a plain pudding. The princesses were taught to be careful with their clothing; kid gloves, after being worn, had to be blown so that the fingers would not lose their shape; bonnet ribbons had to be neatly rolled so that they would appear uncreased when next used; and ribbons from the Queen's discarded hats were ironed and handed on to tie around the brims of the children's.

When the Queen celebrated her birthday in May 1860 she felt that such happiness must go on for ever . . . The weather was exceptionally fine, and nightingales sang 'all round the house'. Musicians played on the terrace, and there was dancing and merriment as there had been nine years ago [on completion of the Household Wing].

Arnold Florance, Queen Victoria at Osborne, (1977)

The Island's Royal Wedding

The marriage of Princess Beatrice to Prince Henry of Battenberg in July 1885 was a happy outcome following a tense period during which Queen Victoria had learned that Beatrice and Henry were in love and wished to marry. The prospect of losing her last child, and, more importantly, her constant companion, so alarmed Queen Victoria that for six months she refused to speak to her daughter and only communicated with notes. It was only when she understood that Prince Henry was willing to make his home with her that she gave them her blessing. In fact, her son-in-law proved to be a tactful, understanding and cheerful man whose influence on Queen Victoria made for a happy household. Princess Beatrice herself made a public commitment to the Isle of Wight when she decided that her wedding should take place in her parish church at Whippingham, a unique and original decision.

Many guests were coming down by train from London for the ceremony, returning that evening, and the problem of seating became difficult. With energy the Lord Chamberlain's Department and Canon Prothero, Rector of Whippingham, set about their task of improvisation and decoration. A passageway, roofed with canvas, was erected from the gate to the entrance of the church, and benches, in tiers were built up on either side of the path, To avoid inconvenience, and possible danger, of the existing steps, a wooden floor was laid down from the porch to the chancel.

The decoration of the church was a matter which occupied the particular attention of the Canon. For the great day he was determined that St. Mildred's should look its best. To be married was not only the daughter of the Queen, but a parishioner and a regular member of his congregation since her childhood days. In this connection he was fortunate to have a co-operative Lord Chamberlain.

The final result proved a triumph for the Canon and the gardeners. Evergreens, lightened with lilies and roses, wreathed the gate. Inside the church lilies and roses also predominated, and the gardeners skilfully erected walls of greenery and colour, and cones of hothouse plants.

The service was to be taken by the Archbishop of Canterbury, assisted by the Bishop of Winchester, the Dean of Windsor and Canon Prothero. The organist and the choir were to be imported from Windsor, and a pointer to the strained resources of Osborne and Whippingham was that a message had to be sent to the organist that no refreshments would be available for the boys. who would have to be fed somewhere on route . . .

The guests came to an island garlanded with flowers and decorations. Sailing craft of all types speckled the Bay, flags and streamers playing in the breeze. Hotels and clubs were in rivalry to proffer the brightest display and everywhere the letters 'B' and 'H' could be seen entwined in flowers. Stands were being run up along the bridal route and fields opened as parking places for carriages. The one essential ingredient needed to ensure the success of the day was the continuance of the fine weather, and in this regard Princess Beatrice shared her mother's good fortune. As a lady-in-waiting once said, if the Queen was to visit a town where it had been raining solidly for days, the sun would come out as her train pulled into the station. So it was 'Queen's weather' on 23 July 1885.

Princess Beatrice's wedding dress was of white satin, trimmed with orange blossom and lace, the lace overskirt held by bouquets of the blossom entwined with white heather. There was lace, too, on the pointed neckline and on the sleeves, for the princess was a lover of, and expert on lace.

Knowing her daughter's love of lace, the Queen now bestowed a signal favour on her. She allowed Princess Beatrice to wear the Honiton lace which she herself had worn on her wedding day forty five full years away. It was a very precious possession to the Queen, and Princess Beatrice was the only one of her daughters to be given the opportunity to wear it [as her veil]. The Queen's wedding dress had also been of white satin trimmed with orange blossom . . .

All the way along the quiet country road carriages were parked in adjoining fields, and the hedge tops showed smiling faces and waving hands. From the crowded stands near the church a great cheer went up as the procession came into sight.

The music broke out, drowning the acclamation, and the four Chamberlains began their reverse steps up the aisle. On her left was the Queen, wearing the new dress which she had ordered for the occasion. On her right was the Prince of Wales, in the uniform of a Field Marshal. Calmly did the Queen give her daughter away, and watch her kneel beside Prince Henry before the altar. There was no trace of the sadness shown on her face at other Royal weddings. This time she knew, in truth, that she was not losing a daughter, but gaining a son.

'At 5,' the Duke of Connaught wrote in his diary, 'we saw the young couple drive off for their honeymoon to Lady Cochrane's Villa [Quarr Abbey House] near Ryde . . . We all dined in uniform in the two large tents. The Queen was again present and seemed wonderfully cheerful and well. The gardens were beautifully illuminated and the Hector and the Royal Yacht, besides being illuminated, gave a very pretty display of fireworks.'

David Duff, The Shy Princess, (1958)

15 · THE POET LAUREATE

Alfred Lord Tennyson's first visit to the Island was made in 1846 four years before his marriage to Emily Sellwood and the attraction remained with him. When he and his wife were looking for a home in the country in 1853 Tennyson returned to the Island, he saw Farringford near Freshwater Bay and thought it worthwhile Emily coming to see it. When she looked at the view from the drawing room window, she thought, 'I must have that view', told her husband, and the matter was settled. On 25 November she, Tennyson and their baby son Hallam were rowed across from Lymington and their life in the Island began.

1853 November 25th

A great day for us. We reached Farringford. It was a misty morning & two of the servants on seeing it burst into tears saying they could never live in such a lonely place. We amused ourselves during the autumn and winter by sweeping up leaves for exercise and by making a muddy path thro' the plantation into a Sandy one. We were delighted with the snowdrops and primroses in the plantation & by the cooing of the Stock-dove & the song of the Redwings.

Richard J. Hutchings and Brian Hinton ed., The Farringford Journal of Emily Tennyson 1853 – 1864

Life at Farringford quickly settled into a distinctive rhythm – giving Tennyson the pattern and order he craved for but he had never been able to realize during their days at Twickenham. He would normally breakfast alone and then spend half an hour in meditation over his first pipe of the day. Then he would work and break off for a long two-hour walk before lunch. In the afternoon there would be another long two-hour walk, with dinner taken between five and six, (the meal would invariably be a roast, followed by apple pie. In one regard at least, Tennyson was typically Victorian – his diet.) This was followed by another solitary pipe – the umpteenth of the day – and by port-drinking and further work. Then he would come down and read aloud and talk until late.

There were, then, three working periods in his study during the day. One in the morning soon after breakfast; one in the afternoon soon after lunch, and the last in the evening immediately after supper. But much of his initial composition was done, as had long been his habit, while out walking, and the earliest draft of a poem would be a simple transcription of what had already been written in his head. The first two sessions at his desk were devoted mainly to reading and thinking. It was in the evening that he spent some time working over his poetry.

Nathaniel Hawthorne, the American writer, when he saw Tennyson for the first time wrote a vivid description of the poet.

'Tennyson is the most picturesque figure, without affectation, that I ever saw; of middle size, rather slouching, dressed entirely in black, and with nothing white about him except the collar of his shirt, which methought might have been clean the day before. He had on a black wide-awake hat, with round crown and wide irregular brim, beneath which came down his long black hair, looking terribly tangled; he had a long pointed beard, too, a little browner than the hair, and not so abundant as to incumber any of the expression of his face . . . His face was very dark, and not exactly a smooth face, but worn, and expressing great sensitiveness . . . I heard his voice; a bass voice, but not of resounding depth; a voice rather broken, as it were, and ragged about the edges, but pleasant to the ear.

Michael Thorne, Tennyson, (*1992*)

'Maud' Pays for Farringford

Although there were many adverse criticisms of Maud, the poem sold quite well, and with the proceeds Tennyson was at last able to buy Farringford. On April 30th, 1856, Mrs. Tennyson wrote happily in her journal:

'We have agreed to buy, so I suppose this ivied home among the pine -trees is ours. Went to our withy holt: such beautiful blue hyacinths, orchises, primroses, daisies, marsh-marigolds and cuckoo-flowers. Wild cherry trees too with single snowy blossom, and the hawthorns white with their 'pearls of May'. The park has for many days been rich with cowslips and furze in bloom. The elms are a golden wreath at the foot of the Down ; to the north of the house the mespilus and horse-chestnut are in flower and the apple trees are covered with rosy buds. A. [Alfred] dug the bed ready for the rhododendrons. A thrush was singing among the nightingales and other birds, as he said, 'mad with joy'. At sunset, the golden green of the trees, the burning splendour of Blackgang Chine and St. Catherine's, and the red bank of the primeval river, contrasted with the turkis-blue of the sea (that is our view from the drawing-room), make altogether a miracle of beauty. We are glad that Farringford is ours.'

Richard J. Hutchings, Idylls of Farringford, (1965)

Maud *was Tennyson's first major work as Poet Laureate, a dark poem which draws on his own experience of rebuffs and sadnesses. It was written at Farringford during the harsh winter of 1854-55 and was a work that remained specially dear to him. The spark that gave light to the poem had been written many years earlier in 1833-34 but had been put away. It was the unexpected discovery of these lines by his friend Sir John Simeon of Swainston, Calbourne, that rekindled in Tennyson the urge to work on it. Sir John's daughter remembered the event and wrote of it later in the century.*

The writing and publication of Maud were largely due to my father. Looking through some papers one day at Farringford with his friend, he came across the exquisite lyric 'that 'twere possible,' and said, 'Why do you keep these beautiful lines unpublished?' Mr Tennyson told him that

it was really intended for a dramatic poem which he had never been able to carry out. My father gave him no peace till he persuaded him to set about the poem, and not very long after he put 'Maud' into his hands.
Agnes Grace Weld, Glimpses of Tennyson, (*1903*)

The verses that closed the first part of Maud – 'Come into the garden Maud' – became the Victorian poem, read and recited throughout the English-speaking world. In the Island it is associated with the garden at Swainston and certainly the description in verse six is an accurate description of the landscape near the house. Tennyson was a frequent visitor to Swainston and the scenery would be part of his imaginative store, so the local belief may well have credibility.

Maud; A Monodrama

Come into the garden, Maud,
    For the black bat, night, has flown,
Come into the garden, Maud,
    I am here at the gate alone;
And the woodbine spices are wafted abroad,
    And the musk of the rose is blown.

And the soul of the rose went into my
    blood,
    And the music clash'd in the hall;
And long by the garden lake I stood,
    For I heard your rivulet fall
From the lake to the meadow and on to the
    wood,
    Our wood, that is dearer than all;
Ed. T. Herbert Warren, Tennyson, Poems and Plays, (*1971*)

Tennyson had come to Freshwater for peace and quiet but he became very much a public personality, troubled with intrusive sightseers. His daily walk over High Down had to be protected and for this he took his own measures, but even so curious tourists found bold ways to gaze on their hero.

Bayard Taylor . . . gives an account of a walk with Tennyson . . . 'We climbed the steep coomb of the chalk cliff and slowly wandered westward till we reached the Needles. During the conversation with which we beguiled the way, I was struck with the variety of the Poet's knowledge; not a little flower on the Down which the sheep had spared escaped his notice, and the geology of the coast, both terrestrial and submarine, was perfectly familiar to him.'

. . . the Poet built the bridge over Tennyson Lane to escape from his admirers. It still stands as he made it, so that by crossing the bridge, he could avoid the crowds who would gather at the green door in the lane, on the chance of seeing the Poet come out for his daily walk. After hours of waiting, all that could be seen by the public was a flash of the Poet's cloak and hat, as, with bent head, he raced across the bridge from his garden to 'The Wilderness' and from thence on to the Down.

Hester Thackeray Fuller, Three Freshwater Friends, *(1936)*

. . . when Holman Hunt was staying at Farringford, he and Tennyson were coming back from their morning walk and saw a group of apparently inoffensive people standing near the gate. Quickly Tennyson led him the long way round to the house, escaping their observation. He told Hunt that often, working in the garden, he would hear voices saying, 'There he is – look,' and half a dozen Cockney heads would appear in a row over the wall, staring intently. Once an intruder got into the garden, and as they were sitting at luncheon he flattened his nose against the window, crying, 'You can see him well from here.' Tennyson exaggerated the extent to which he was spied upon, but the annoyance was surely considerable. As always, he was divided in his reactions: furious if stared at, worried if he were paid no attention.

Robert Bernard Martin, The Unquiet Heart, *(1980)*

Finally the summer at Farringford became too much and a summer retreat had to be found where they could escape the height of the season, but they always returned to the Island in the autumn and they enjoyed the best months of the year before leaving again at the end of June.

Tennyson to the Duke of Argyll

Stoatley Farm, Haslemere

My Dear Duke,

. . . We are at present lodging at a farmhouse here in the neighbourhood of Haslemere. My wife has always had a fancy for the sandy soil and heather-scented air of this part of England, and we are intending to buy a few acres, and build a little home here, whither we may escape when the cockneys are running over my lawns at Freshwater.

1868. On January 31st my father left, by way of Winchester, for Haslemere, to fix the site of the new house [Aldworth] on Blackdown.
Hallam Tennyson, Alfred Lord Tennyson - A Memoir, (1905)

Julia Margaret Cameron - The Tennysons' Neighbour

Mrs. Cameron moved to Freshwater in 1860 to be near the Tennysons and when she was able to buy two small houses in Terrace Lane she was no more than a few yards from their house, a close and somewhat overwhelming neighbour. She is remembered today for the photographs she took and developed at Dimbola, the house she created from her original two purchases. Tennyson was among the first studies she made, but no one was safe from her energetic demands. She began as an amateur having only the most primitive conditions in which to work with dangerous chemicals; she succeeded in breaking the mould of earlier photography and established it as an art form.

Colin Ford in his preface to Immortal Faces *describes the technical problems she faced.*

Julia Margaret Cameron lived the sort of life in which she need never make a bed or boil an egg. Yet she took up photography in an era when it could not have been more cumbersome or dangerous. She had to mix/make her own chemicals (including gun cotton, a volatile explosive);

spread them evenly on a large sheet of spotlessly clean glass; and take a picture before the sensitive formula had dried out.

The likelihood of such an eccentric, wayward, untidy woman overcoming these technical difficulties to create some of the greatest portraits of the nineteenth century – in any medium – seems remote. Yet, miraculously, that is exactly what she did.

The great experiment began with a gift from her daughter.

My first lens was given me by my cherished daughter with the words, 'it may amuse you, Mother, to try to photograph during your solitude at Freshwater.'

I handled my lens with a tender ardour, and it has become to me a living thing, with voice and memory and creative vigour. I began with no knowledge of the art. I did not know where to place my dark box, how to focus my sitter and my first picture I effaced to my consternation by rubbing my hand over the filmy side of the glass. I turned my coal-house into my dark room and a glazed fowl-house I had given to my children became my glass house. The society of hens and chickens was soon changed for that of poets, prophets, painters and lovely maidens, who all in turn have immortalised this humble little farm erection.

Hester Fuller writes of Mrs Cameron,

Mrs Cameron followed her art with extraordinary trouble and devotion, and also expected as much from her sitters. Sitting to her was a serious affair not to be lightly entered upon. Her sitters came at her summons, they trembled, or would have trembled, could they have dared, when the round black eye of the camera was turned upon them. They felt what consequences, what disastrous waste of time and money and effort might ensue from any passing quiver of emotion. For in those days Mrs Cameron had to make her own plates, and her sitters would have to sit without moving for ten minutes while the cap was off the lens.

Laura Gurney, one of her young models, recalls her as 'a strange and wilful creature, and a law unto herself'. To me, I frankly own, she appeared as a terrifyingly elderly woman, short and squat, with none of the Pattle grace and beauty about her, though more than her fair share of their passionate energy and wilfulness. Dressed in dark clothes, stained with chemicals from the photography (and smelling of them, too), with a plump eager face and piercing eyes and a voice husky, and a little harsh, yet in some way compelling and even charming, my first sight of her was in her studio at Dimbola, the little cottage home at Freshwater, about a quarter of a mile from the sea; and immediately we, Rachel and I, were pressed into the services of the camera. Our roles were no less than those of two of the angels of the Nativity, and to sustain them we were scantily clad, and each had a pair of heavy swan's wings fastened to her narrow shoulders, while Aunt Julia, with ungentle hand, touzled our hair to get rid of its prim nursery look.

No wonder those old photographs of us, leaning over imaginary ramparts of heaven, look anxious and wistful. This is how we felt, for we never knew what Aunt Julia was going to do next, nor did anyone else for the matter of that. All we were conscious of was that once in her clutches we were perfectly helpless. 'Stand there', she shouted, and we stood there for hours, if necessary, gazing at the model of the Heavenly Babe (in reality a sleeping child deposited in a property manger). The parents, anxious and uneasy, were outside, no more able to rescue their infant until Aunt Julia had finished with it, than we should have been . . .

No-one had ever undertaken a real portrait study until Aunt Julia with her hobby and her unconventiality, revolutionised all previous ideas upon the subject by producing, though in a rough and ready state, what in reality were works of art.

Brian Hinton, Immortal Faces, (1992)

16 . TIMES AND SEASONS

We begin with a science fiction story. John Wyndham's novel The Day of the Triffids *is a story of fortitude in surviving a catastrophic astronomical event which causes most of the population to become instantly blind. Triffids had been grown to extract valuable oils and juices highly nutritious for stock feeding. The plants could walk, communicate between themselves and had a sting which could kill. While carefully managed they were no danger but with a blind population the way was open for them to advance. Small groups of survivors did establish themselves and one group in Oxfordshire realized that they needed to move to a more secure area. One of the party told his story to another family group in West Sussex.*

Clearly, the best self-maintaining defence line would be water. To that end they had held a discussion on the relative merits of various islands. It had been chiefly climate that had decided them in favour of the Isle of Wight, despite some misgivings over the area that would have to be cleared. Accordingly, in the following March they had packed up and moved on.

'When we got there', Ivan said, 'the triffids seemed even thicker than where we'd left. No sooner had we begun to settle ourselves in a big country house near Godshill than they started collecting along the walls in thousands. We let 'em come for a couple of weeks or so, then we went for 'em with the flame throwers.

'After we'd wiped that lot out, we let them accumulate again, and then we blitzed 'em once more – and so on. We could afford to do it properly there, because once we were clear of them, we'd not need to use the throwers any more. There could only be a limited number in the island and the more of them that came round us to be wiped out, the better we liked it.'

We had to do it a dozen times before there was any appreciable effect. All round the walls we had a belt of charred stumps before they began to get shy. There were a devil of a lot more of them than we expected.'

'There used to be at least half a dozen nurseries breeding high quality plants in the island – not to mention the private and park ones', I said.

'That doesn't surprise me. There might have been a hundred nurseries by the look of it! . . . Still, we managed to thin down the crowd round our walls after a bit . . . so then we started going out to hunt them instead of just letting them come to us. Between us we covered every inch of the island – or thought we did. By the time we were through, we reckoned we'd put paid to every one in the place, big and small. Even so, some managed to appear the next year, and the year after that. Now we have an intensive search every spring on account of seeds blowing over from the mainland, and settle them right away. While that was going on we were getting organized. There were some fifty or sixty of us to begin with. I took flips in the helicopter, and when I saw signs of a group anywhere, I'd go down and issue a general invitation to come along.'

'. . . Does this mean you're inviting us all to your island haven?' Dennis asked.

'Well, to come on mutual approval, at least', Ivan replied ' . . . We aren't out to reconstruct – we want to build something new and better . . . The best way to learn about us is to come and find out. If you like us, you'll stay – but even if you don't, I think you'll find the Channel Isles is a better spot than this is likely to be a few years from now. . . .'

Our hopes all centre here now . . . So we must regard the task ahead as ours alone. We think now we can see the way, but there is still a lot of work and research to be done before the day when we, or our children, or their children, will cross the narrow straits on the great crusade to drive the triffids back and back with ceaseless destruction until we have wiped the last of them from the face of the land they have usurped.

John Wyndham, The Day of the Triffids, (1954)

New Year's Day

A custom is still retained at Yarmouth of the children singing on the first day of the year, Wassall or Wessell, from the Saxon 'Health to you'.

Wassall, Wassall, to our town,
The cup is white and the ale is brown;
The cup is made of the ashen tree,
And so is the ale of good barley;
Little maid, little maid, turn the pin,
Open the door, and let me in;
God be here, and God be there!
We wish you all a happy new year.

A.G. *Cole*, Yarmouth Isle of Wight, (*1946*)

Easter Bank Holiday

The Tea Garden is still so much part of the holiday scene that it is no surprise to find it included in a novel set in the Island. A kindly but wry appreciation looks behind the scene of a family business.

We were waiting in the garden room of Seven Dwarfs Tea Garden to see what colour scheme Father had decreed this year for the little metal tables and the seven plaster dwarfs which ornamented the garden in privet niches. As soon as we had been told, we should start painting and the new season would have begun. . . .

'Six Doc's Doughnuts, six Dopey's Delight and a plate of sandwiches', I intoned, scribbling on my little pad though I refused to wear any sort of waitress' uniform. The party nodded happily, in Bank Holiday mood, content to gaze out on dwarfs and garden from the deceptive warmth of the sun parlour with its spread of red-white-and blue tables. Easter Monday teas were in full swing. . . .

'Mother, six more Delights, please.'

Father skipped in, waving his camera, white curls artistically wild above pointed ears, a pixie among dwarfs, blue eyes full of glee.

'Got to put in another film. I've taken sixteen already – sixteen at half a crown each, think of that.'

He shut himself into the broom cupboard cum dark room.

'Did you put the bottle gardens on a front table?' Mother demanded fretfully, slapping pink jelly into bowls for the Delights.

'Of course, darling. We've sold three – one more and you will have beaten Father hollow.'

I made the twenty-first pot of tea and went swanning back, overhearing from one table, 'Oh yes, we always come on Easter Monday – such a sweet family don't you think?' . . .

'How much are those interesting bottle gardens?' asked Pink Hat. Her handbag was real pigskin.

'Seventeen and six pence,' I risked.

'Oh. My friend bought one from you on Good Friday and it was only twelve and six.' Probably that woman in the scuffed canvas shoes.

'Of course, there are cheaper ones with fewer plants,' I said disdainfully, moving away towards Check Cap who wanted his bill and the family of six who needed hot water.

'Ten shillings, please.'

By six o'clock all the bottle gardens were sold, Father had taken twenty Happy snaps, and only three visitors still lingered among the stained and crumby tricolour tables.

Patricia Sibley, A Far Cry from Clammergoose, (1971)

Shrove Tuesday

When I was quite a small child all the school children were let out early at dinner time on Shrove Tuesday – of course to go shroving. First we went to 'Veniscombe' where the Misses Hargrove lived, then to the Shop, where Mr John Wheeler the baker lived, on to 'The Pointer Inn' and finally to the Vicarage. We sang a little ditty which went:

> Shroven, shroven, here we come a-shroven,
> A piece of bread, a piece of cheese, a piece of your fat bacon.
> The roads are very dirty, my boots are very clean,
> I've got a little pocket to put my penny in.

We were rewarded with money (coppers) and boiled sweets which were thrown and we scrambled for them when we had to watch out we didn't get our fingers trodden on.

Mrs. Margaret Lale, Newchurch Remembered, Newchurch Women's Institute (1988)

May Day at Yarmouth

[An] old custom of the year, long since died out, was on May Day, when
little girls, prettily dressed in light summer frocks, would carry garlands
of wild flowers round the town, and, stopping at nearly every door
would chant:
  'Oh, the first of May is Garland Day,
  So please to remember the Garland, the Garland,
  Oh, please to remember the Garland.'
And there were few householders who did not cheerfully comply.
A.G. *Cole,* Yarmouth Isle of Wight, *(1946)*

Danger in the Hay Fields

The Turkish pirates of Algiers have done many robberies on the coast, .
. . the west countrymen dare not peep forth for fear of them. On the Isle
of Wight they took men and women making hay insomuch as they said
they liked English women so well that before they departed they would
have every man one.
ed. Maija Jansson & William B. Bidwell, Proceedings in Parliament 1625, *(1987)*

The 1970 Pop Festival

*The Pop Festival at Afton near Freshwater made the Island
internationally famous. The overwhelming number of young people who
crammed into west Wight taxed to the limit the local authority and the
transport services – and the sound levels taxed the ears of Freshwater
and its neighbourhood. Brian Hinton, who was later to become a
permanent resident, was among the fans and later looked back on that
remarkable weekend.*

I drive past the 1970 Festival site most days. It's under cultivation now,
a vast plain rich in wheat and barley. The only human constituents of the
scene are the occasional farm worker hidden in his tractor or a lone
windsurfer hanging motionless over Afton Down. And yet half a million
people once made this their home, stretched as far as the eye could see

in a kaleidoscope of colour and excitement. British Rail subsequently announced that over 600,000 people had used their ferries during the Festival period.

Record Mirror *painted the scene in prose of violent day-glo;*

'Beaming light towers like prison camp spires lent electric lustre to freaking patrons who appeared and disappeared suddenly from forests of hair. They floated and hopped like midnight maidens set upon midnight madness, roving in and out of the fluorescent cigarette smoke . . . Just over the hill was the rich green sea where afternoons saw young sirens bouncing in the waves, their chests bulging free in the summer surf . . .

Saturday night extended into Sunday morning and the arrival on stage of 'The Who'..

And now – a nice rock band from Shepherds Bush - the 'Oo', said Jeff Dexter, and one of the great groups of our time ran on stage . . . They must have played for three, maybe four hours. They started at one o'clock on Sunday morning, and by the time they were finished it was nearly dawn. *The Who's* performance was the high spot of the Festival for most people . . .

The Who played on well after 4am and at quarter past four came a thrilling moment when they turned huge spotlights on the crowd from backstage, lighting up the masses, including a flurry of moths, leaping like loons in the vastness . . .

Sunday morning saw thousands of bleak faces, punch drunk with tiredness . . . The ground was an obstacle course of beer cans, cups, paper and colourful garbage of all sorts mixed with rich brown mud . . . Monday saw a Dunkirk evacuation of the Island as the site turned into – the longest bus queue we had ever seen; two queues wound for about a mile from camp sites on opposite sides of the arena, but the wet and windswept fans shifted slowly forward in surprisingly patient and orderly fashion.'

Brian Hinton, Message to Love – the Isle of Wight Festivals 1968-70, *(1995)*

Newport Hiring Fair

After earning my 20 shillings in October, I went to Newport for a
holiday on what was termed bargain Saturday. The three Saturdays
before Michaelmas were the days when it was customary for the farmers
to come to Newport to hire their servants, being termed the first, middle
and third bargain Saturdays. The bargains generally took place in one of
the markets or beneath the Town Hall, and were generally made for a
year, with both sexes represented. These Saturdays were very popular
with the country lads and lasses, who came into Newport from all parts
of the Island arrayed in their best. The young men mostly wore blue
short sailors' jackets, with rows of buttons each side, a coloured or black
neckerchief, a cotton shirt with blue stripes and high collar, sometimes a
red waist coat with black spots and pearl buttons, drab corduroy
trousers, and a light pair of homemade lace-up boots, a broad brimmed
hat, and a bandanna handkerchief in the jacket. The lasses were addicted
to ribbons, lace, bright coloured cotton prints, some with waist ribbands
and low shoes. The townspeople called them 'Jans and Marys'.'
Mark William Norman ed. Vincent Chambers, Old Men Remember, *(1988)*

The Christmas Play

The performers were generally young men of the neighbourhood, who,
during the Christmas holidays, perambulated their own and adjoining
parishes, exhibiting in the houses of the gentry and principal persons;
and a performance open to all comers at the village inn, generally
finished each evening.

Father and Mother Christmas appear in old great coats, the latter
wearing an old bonnet and skirt. They walk in bending, and as if
decrepit through age, with the backs of their coats well stuffed with
straw. This is necessary as during the performance they furiously
belabour each other, Father Christmas wielding a cudgel, and Mother
Christmas a formidable broom. 'Poor and Mean' appears in tattered
habiliments; 'The Doctor' in a rusty black coat and wig; the 'Valiant
Soldier' in an old red uniform coat; the 'Turkish Knight' wears a Turban,
and has generally a good deal of green in his attire; 'King George' is
resplendent in a shining helmet and a coat covered in spangles; the

'Noble Captain' often sports a cocked hat and blue coat; and the dresses of most of the players are profusely bedecked with tinsel and ribbons of different colours according to their fancy.

The play is spoken in Isle of Wight dialect.

> Here comes I – the Turkish knight
> In Turkish land I've learned to fight
> I'll fight King George and all his min,
> And taame their courage bold; . . .
> I'd hag him, I'd jag him,
> I'd cut him as small as a fly.
> I'd zend him to zome far land
> To make a Crismus pie.

> Here come I – King George,
> That man of courage bold,
> And with my soord and spear
> I've won ten crowns of gold.
> I fout the viery dragon
> And brought him gurt to slaughter,
> And by the meeans o' that I won
> The King of Egypt's daughter.

Aston A. Long, Dialect of the Isle of Wight with Tales and Anecdotes, *(1931)*

The Island at War

During 1940 families all over the country tuned in their wireless sets on Sunday evenings to hear a seven minute talk that followed the nine o'clock news bulletin. The speaker was J.B. Priestly, then living in Billingham Manor, between Chillerton and Chale Green and one of his earliest talks was a description of how the local community was responding to the war. No places could be identified but the nature of the Island shines out.

Sunday, 16th June 1940
A night or two ago, I had my first spell with our Local Defence Volunteers or 'Parashots.' I'd been on the muster for the previous fortnight - but I'd been away, busy with other work, so I hadn't been able

to see how our village was keeping watch and ward. Ours is a small and scattered village, but we'd had a fine response to the call for Volunteers; practically every able-bodied man in the place takes his turn. The post is on top of a high down, with a fine view over a dozen wide parishes. The men I met up there the other night represented a good cross-section of English rural life; we had a parson, a bailiff, a builder, farmers and farm labourers. Even the rarer and fast disappearing rural trades were represented – for we had a hurdle maker there; and his presence, together with that of a woodman and a shepherd, made me feel sometimes that I'd wandered into one of those rich chapters of Thomas Hardy's fiction in which his rustics meet in the gathering darkness on some Wessex hillside. And indeed there was something in the preliminary talk, before the sentries were posted for the night, that gave this whole horrid business of air raids and threatened invasion a rustic, homely, almost comfortable atmosphere, and really made a man feel more cheerful about it. In their usual style, these country chaps called every aeroplane 'she'. They'd say: 'Ay, she come along through the gap and over by Little Witchett – as I see with my own eyes. Then searchlights picks her up – might be Black Choine way or farther along, over boi Colonel Wilson's may be – an Oi says to Tarm; 'Won't be long now, you'll see afore they get her – and then, bingo, masters, down she come!' They have the sound countryman's habit of relating everything intimately to their own familiar background. Now of course this doesn't take away any of the real menace, but what it does do is somehow to put all this raiding and threatened invasion in their proper places. The intellectual is apt to see these things as the lunatic end of everything, as part of a crazy Doomsday Eve, as he goes about moaning, or runs away to America. But the simple and saner countryman sees this raiding and invading as the latest manifestation of that everlasting menace which he always has to fight – sudden blizzards at lambing time, or floods just before the harvest.

I think the countryman knows, without being told, that we hold our lives here as we hold our farms, upon certain terms. One of those terms is that while wars still continue, while one nation is ready to hurl its armed men at another, you must if necessary stand up and fight for your own. And this decision comes from the natural piety of simple but sane men. Such men, you will notice, are happier now than the men who have lost their natural piety.

Well, as we talked on our post on the hilltop, we watched the dusk deepen in the valleys below, where our women-folk listened to the news as they knitted by the hearth, and remembered that these were our homes and that now at any time they might be blazing ruins. The sentries took their posts. There was a mist coming over the down. Nothing much happened for a time. A green light that seemed to defy all blackout regulations turned out to be an extra large and luminous glow-worm; the glow-worms, poor ignorant little creatures, don't know there's a war on and so continue lighting themselves up. A few searchlights went stabbing through the dusk and then faded. The mist thickened, and below in the valleys, there wasn't the faintest glimmer of light. You heard the ceaseless high melancholy singing of the telegraph wires in the wind.

So we talked about what happened in the last war, and about the hay and barley, about beef and milk and cheese and tobacco. The belt of fog over to the left became almost silvery, because somewhere along there all the searchlights were sweeping the sky. Then somewhere beyond that vague silveriness, there was a sound as if gigantic doors were being slammed to. There was the rapid stabbing noise of anti-aircraft batteries, and far away some rapping of machine-guns. Then the sirens went, in our two nearest towns, as if all that part of the darkened countryside, like a vast trapped animal, was screaming at us.

But then the sounds of bombs and gun fire and planes all died away. The 'All Clear' went, and then there was nothing but the misty cool night, drowned in silence, and this handful of us on the hilltop.

I felt up there a powerful and rewarding sense of community; and with it too a feeling of deep continuity. There we were, ploughman and parson, shepherd and clerk, turning out at night, as our forefathers had often done before us, to keep watch and ward over the sleeping English hills and fields and homesteads. I've mentioned Thomas Hardy, whose centenary has just been celebrated. Don't you find in his tales and poems often derived from the talk he listened to as a boy, a sense that Napoleon, with his threatened invasion by the Grand Army at Boulogne, was only just round the corner? And I felt, out in the night on the hilltop, that the watch they kept then was only yesterday; that all this raiding and threat of invasion, though menacing and dangerous enough, was not some horror big enough to split the world - but merely our particular testing time; what we must face, as our forefathers faced such things, in order to enjoy our own again. It would come down upon us; it would be terrible; but it would pass.

J.B. Priestly, Postscripts, (1940)

17 · IN MEMORIAM

The enjoyment of reading memorial tablets and inscriptions on tombstones is long-standing and we can still find delight in them, although many have worn away with the passage of years. Fortunately travellers from earlier centuries noted down their favourites and we can savour them today.

Carisbrooke's Adventurer

William Keeling was a true seventeenth century adventurer, as an agent of the East India company, he made three voyages to what is now Indonesia. On the second he discovered a remote group of coral islands in the Indian Ocean south of Sumatra, now known as the Cocos Keeling Islands. He retired to the Isle of Wight with two Crown appointments, Captain of Cowes Castle and Keeper of the Park, a royal hunting enclosure to the west of Carisbrooke. Here he died, relatively young, remembered by a memorial panel in Carisbrooke church which summarizes his successful life – of less account than his Christian life – and takes him on his final journey to his Holy Land.

Heere lieth the boddy of the right Worthy
William Keeling Esquire Groom of the chamber to
our Soveraigne King James Generall for the East
Indie adventurors whither he was thrice by
them imployd and dyinge in this isle at the age
of 42 An° 1619 Sept, 19, hath this remembrance
heer fixed by his loveing and sorrowfull
     wife Ann Keeling
Fortie and two yeares, in this Vessell fraile
On the Rough seas of life did Keeling saile,
A Merchant Fortunate, a Captaine bould,
A Courtier gratious, yet (Alas) not Old.
Such Wealth, experience, honour & high praise
Few Winne in Twice soe manie daies.
But what the World Amird, he deemed but drosse
For Christ, Without CHRIST all his gaines but losse.
For him and his dear love, with merrie Cheere
To the Holy Land, his last course he did Steere.
Faith servd for Salies the Sacred Word for card
Hope was his Anchor, Glorie his Reward,
And thus with gales of grace, by happie venter
Through straits of Death, heavens harbor he did
    ENTER

*The memorial tablet to Dr. Thomas Pittis in Niton is particular in having
a throw-away clause which reveals a somewhat cavalier attitude to the
Anglican Church he served and a final line which seems to have been
added as an afterthought.*

Here lie deposited, till the resurrection of the just,
    the mortal remains of Dr. Thomas Pittis,
Late Rector of St. Botolph's near Bishopsgate,
    in London.
Who after a life of more than L years,
Spent chiefly in serving the Church of England
    and in praying for it
(when he could no otherwise defend it)
Being consumed of a long sicknesse,

And with zeal for the House of God;
He resigned his soul into the hands of his Saviour
    Dec. 28 MDCLXXXVII
Leaving to men an eminent example of Piety,
    learning, and virtue;
And to God's protection, two sons and two daughters,
    Thomas, William, Elizabeth and Catherine,
Which blessings he had by Mrs. Elizabeth Pittis,
    daughter of William Stephens, Esq.
Who hath consecrated this monument of her sorrow
    to the memory of her most beloved husband,
    supporting her loss
with the assurance of his blessednesse.

The above Dr. Thomas Pittis was a native of this parish.

Godshill

Here lyeth the remains of
Mr William Thornton, Clerk, Rector of this Parish,
    and Minister of Godshill,
Son of the Rev. Mr. Christopher Thornton, in Westmoreland,
      1750
Here the weary may be at rest, they hear not the voice of the
oppressor.

Mr Thornton had maintained a long and tedious lawsuit with the
impropriators of the great tithes of Godshill, in order to obtain the tithe
of milk; but as this was previous to the present mode of proceeding in
the Court of Exchequer, the decision was never given, though the cause
had been pending for nearly all the time Mr. Thornton was vicar of
Godshill, a space of about ten years . . .
The Hampshire Repository 1799 – 1801

In the twentieth century Hubert Poole was a collector of tombstone verses he found in Island churchyards, choosing particularly those associated with trades and occupations.

Carisbrooke

Charle Dixon, blacksmith

> My sledge and hammer lie reclined,
> My bellows too have lost their wind,
> My fire's extinct, my forge decayed,
> My vice all in the dust is laid:
> My coal is spent, my iron gone,
> My last nail's driven, my work is done.

Kingston

Micah Morris, d.1837 aged 67, farmer

> With pain and toil I long did till the ground,
> But in it now a resting place have found:
> Through my Redeemer Jesus Christ I trust
> That I like purest Wheat shall spring from dust
> And share the joyful harvest of the Just.

Godshill

Captain William Grove d. 17th Jan. 1822, aged 59, seaman

> Through Neptune's waves by tempest tos't
> He ploughed for forty years.
> Though twice shipwrecked but never lost
> Nor felt unmanly fears.
> Once he did 'scape a watery grave
> By floating on an oar
> When all the crew beneath the wave
> Went down to rise no more.
> But any means where God shall please
> to cut the mortal thread,
> For he thus saved from raging seas
> Departed in his bed.

Newchurch

Richard Forward d. 1826
    Parish Clerk 54 years
Parish Schoolmaster 53 years
    Church Clerk 24 years
In yonder sacred pile his voice was wont to sound,
    And now his body rests beneath the hallowed ground
He taught the peasant boy to read and use his pen,
    His earthly toils are o'er – he's cried his last Amen.

Arreton

Wilm. Rayner, d. May 15th, 1823, bellringer

Skilled in the mystery of the pleasing Peal
    which few can know and fewer still reveal,
Whether the little bells or Bell sublime,
    To split a moment to the truth of time,
Time so oft truly beat, at length o'er came,
    Yet shall this tribute long preserve his name.

Hubert H. Poole, Come and see my Island. *Typescript held at Lord Louis Library, Newport (1934).*

The piety of the memorials above gives place to aggrieved anger on the gravestone of Thomas Sivell in Binstead, a smuggler shot on his boat when it was challenged by the Revenue officers.

to the memory of Thos Sivell
who was cruely shot on board his
sloop by some officers of the customs
of the Port of Portsmouth on the
15th of June 1785 at the age of 64 years
leaving a disconsolate Widow & family

All you that pass pray look and see
How soon my life was took from me
By those officers as you hear
They spill'd my Blood that was so dear
But GOD is Good is Just and true
And will reward to each their due

Jack Jones, Isle of Wight Curiosities *(1986)*

Shorwell

Barnabas Leigh was unfortunate enough to bury two wives within four years; the first, Elizabeth Bampfield, was the mother of fifteen children and died in March 1615, the second, Gertrude Percevall, died childless in December 1619. Mr. Leigh decided to erect a brass which celebrated both.

Since neither penne nor pencill can set forth
Of these two matchles wives the matchles worth
We're forc't to cover in this silent tombe
The praises of a chaste and fruitful wombe:
And with death's sable vaile in darknes hide,
The ritch rare virtues of a barren bride.
Sweet saintlike paire of soules, in whome did shine
Such models of perfection faeminine,
Such Pietie, love, zeale: That though we sinners
Their lives have lost, yet still [them]selves are winners,
For they secure, heavens happines inherit,
Whilst we lament their losse, admire their merit.

Barbara Jones, The Isle of Wight, *(1950)*

18 · CROSSING THE BAR

In 1889, following a serious illness, Alfred Lord Tennyson wrote what is probably his most famous poem after making the brief passage from Lymington to Yarmouth. His son Hallam described it as 'the crown of your life's work'.

Crossing the Bar

Sunset and evening star,
    And one clear call for me!
And may there be no moaning of the bar,
    When I put out to sea,

But such a tide as moving seems asleep,
    Too full for sound and foam,
When that which drew from out the soundless deep
    Turns again home.

Twilight and evening bell,
    And after that the dark!
And may there be no sadness of farewell,
    When I embark;

For tho' from out our bourne of Time and Place
    The flood may bear me far,
I hope to see my Pilot face to face
    When I have crost the bar.

ACKNOWLEDGEMENTS

I am grateful to authors and publishers for permission to reproduce material which is still in copyright. Where possible I have used extracts in their entirety, but on occasions I have either omitted paragraphs or words within paragraphs.

I would like to thank the following for allowing the inclusion of extracts: from *The Isle of Wight*, Brian Dicks (David & Charles, 1979) by kind permission of the publishers; John Margham & Dr Della Hooke for John Margham's *Charters, landscapes and hides on the Isle of Wight* in *Landscape History* (Society of Landscape Studies); Colin Pope for the extract on Ancient Woodland from *The Isle of Wight Flora* (The Dovecote Press); Paul Hyland for the piece from *Wight, Biography of an Island* (The Dovecote Press); the Royal Historical Society for the two extracts from *The Journal of William Schellinks' Travels in England 1661-1663* edited by Maurice Exwood and H.L. Lehman and the piece from *Religion, Politics, and Society in Sixteenth Century England* edited by Ian W. Archer; Peter Cross (Cross Publishing) for the extracts from Derek Sprake's *Put out the Flag* and Jill Chaney's *Three Weeks in August*; Jack D. Jones for the pieces from *The Isle of Wight 1558-1642* and *The Royal Prisoner*; the family of the late R.J. Eldridge from *Newport Isle of Wight in Bygone Days*; Patricia Sibley for extracts from *The Island from Within – an Anthology* and *A Far Cry from Clammergoose*; The Hogarth Press for F. Bamford's *A Royalists Notebook*; Adlard Coles Nautical (A & C Black Publishers) for *More Joys of Living* by Uffa Fox (Nautical Publishing); for the piece from *The Official Book: The America's Cup Jubilee 2001* written by Kit Hob and edited by Sam Fryer (Notre Voie Ltd); Ian Sherfield (Business by Design) for *East Cowes Castle, The Seat of John Nash, Esq. A Pictorial History*; Cyril Bainbridge's *Pavilions on the Sea, A History of the Seaside Pleasure Pier* reproduced by permission of Pollinger Limited and the Proprieter; Pan Macmillan for the extract from Philip Norman's *Babycham Night*; the Estate of Lindsay Boynton for the piece from *Georgian and Victorian Shanklin – a pictorial history*; Curtis Brown on behalf of Flora Fraser for *Maud: The Diaries of Maud Berkeley* Copyright © Flora Fraser 1985; E.F. Laidlaw for permission to use the extract from *The Story of the Royal National Hospital Ventnor*: Edward Stanford Ltd for allowing the use of a piece from David and Joan Hay's *The Solent from the Sea*; John Scott Hughes *Harbours of the Solent*; Coach House Publications Ltd 1995 for the

piece from *Alum Bay and the Needles* by John C. Medland MSc; the Estate
of Fred Mew for an extract from *Back of the Wight*; The Dovecote Press for
Oliver Fraser's piece from *The Natural History of the Isle of Wight* and J.
Meade Falkner's *Moonfleet* extract; Mrs R.W.S. Orr for the extract from
Esmé Wingfield-Stratford's *Before the lamps went out*; J. Parsloe for G.
Parsloe's *A Present from Seaview*; Countryside Books and the Isle of Wight
Federation of Women's Institutes for the pieces from *Isle of Wight within
Living Memory*; Win Hollis and the Brighstone Village Museum Trust for
Brighstone Village Isle of Wight; Ian Allen Publishing Ltd (Oxford
Publishing Company) for Andrew Britton's *Once upon a Line vol 2*;
Reproduced by kind permission of the publisher, from *Insula Vecta*, by S.F.
Hockey, published in 1982 by Phillimore & Co Ltd, Shopwyke Manor Barn,
Chichester, West Sussex PO20 2BG; Mabel Roach's daughter for the extract
from *Brighstone Village, Isle of Wight*; Newchurch Women's Institute for
the extracts from *Newchurch Remembered*; Dina Broughton for the piece
from Robert Cassell's *An Eventful Life*; Robin Ford for allowing use of the
poem 'The Sweepboy at Northcourt' from his collection *South*; Brasseys
(Conway Maritime Press) for the piece from Rear-Admiral D. Foster's *At
War With The Smugglers*; The Isle of Wight Council for allowing us to use
an extract from Vicky Badford's *Historic Parks and Gardens of the Isle of
Wight*; The Isle of Wight Natural History and Archaeological Society for Bill
Shepard's *Newport Isle of Wight Remembered*: Collins and Brown for Judy
Johnson and Susan Berry's *English Private Gardens*; Reproduced from
Albert, Uncrowned King by Stanley Weintraub (Copyright © Stanley
Weintraub 1997) by permission of PFD (www.pfd.co.uk) on behalf of
Professor Stanley Weintraub; Chapman & Hall for Winslow Ames' *Prince
Albert and Victorian Taste*; Arnold Florance's sister for the extract from
Queen Victoria at Osborne; David Duff for the extract from *The Shy
Princess*; Little, Brown and Company for Michael Thorne's piece from
Tennyson; Elizabeth Hutchings for the extract from Richard J. Hutchings'
Idylls of Farringford; the poem *Maud; A Monodrama* comes from
Tennyson, Poems and Plays (Oxford University Press); also by permission of
Oxford University Press *Tennyson: the Unquiet Heart* by Robert Bernard
Martin (1980); Brian Hinton for the piece from *Immortal Faces*; David
Higham Associates for the extract from John Wyndham's *The Day of the
Triffids*; Sanctuary Publishing Ltd for Brian Hinton's *Message to Love – the
Isle of Wight Festivals 1968-70*; Ventnor Local History Society for Vincent
Chambers' *Old Men Remembered*; the extract reproduced from *Postscripts*
by J.B. Priestley (Copyright © Estate of J.B. Priestley 1940) by permission of
PFD (www.pfd.co.uk) on behalf of the Estate of J.B. Priestley.

The publishers have endeavoured to contact all holders of copyright, but
will be pleased to correct any omissions or errors in future editions.